JARI EMBROIDERY

Delhi-110052

E-mail: kalpaz@hotmai[illegible]

Phone: 9212729499

Laser Typesetting by: Quick Media, Delhi

Printed at: Singhal Print Media, Delhi

JARI EMBROIDERY

A Study of a Traditional Craft and the Craftsmen of Bengal

Sekh Rahim Mondal

KALPAZ

Jari Embroidery

Rs. 540

ISBN: 978-81-7835-737-9

Published in 2009 in India by
Kalpaz Publications
C-30, Satyawati Nagar,
Delhi-110052
E-mail: kalpaz@hotmail.com
Phone : 9212729499

Laser Typesetting by: Quick Media, Delhi

Printed at : Singhal Print Media, Delhi

DEDICATED
TO

My Mother
Rejia Begum

My Wife
Dr. Begum Rokiya Kohinoor

&

My Son
Raunak Rony

Contents

List of Tables

Preface

In order to retain the relevance in the first changing world, the Social Scientific researches have started to play a new role in the protection and conservation of cultural diversity and documentation of indigenous knowledge system. Traditional arts and crafts have been the very core of Indian civilization. *Jari* work is a kind of hand embroidery and an important artistic craft of this country. It is one such home industry and small-scaled entrepreneurship which has a long tradition in India. But the research studies on this artistic craft producers are very negligible.

Present research is an attempt to examine the social framework of embroidery (*Jari*) work and to assess the socio-economic life of the embrodiders on the basis of information collected from four villages of four different police stations of the district of Howrah in West Bengal. The various problems of this artistic craft and the craft producers, especially of the child labourers have been highlighted in this research. The empirical study was conducted by the author during the period 1998 to 2000. The study contains rich qualitative and quantitative facts relevant for policy formation.

This study is based on minor research project titled—"The Embroidery (*Jari*) Works and the Embroiders of Bengal : An Anthropological Study of a Traditional Craft and an Occupational Group, with Special Reference to its Child Labour", sponsored by Indian Council of Social-Science Research, New Delhi in 1997. I am, therefore, grateful to ICSSR for assigning me this task of study by releasing the research grant. The research study was conducted under the

University of North Bengal (NBU) where I am associated since 1981. I gratefully acknowledge the help and co-operation of several officials of ICSSR and NBU for completion of this research work.

I pay my deepest gratitude to Prof. R.G. Mukherjee and Prof. P.K. Saha, the former Vice-Chancellors of the University of North Bengal for their valuable help and sympathy to conduct and to complete this study. In this context I also like to express my deep sense of gratitude to Prof. A. Basumajumdar the present Vice-Chancellor of the University of North Bengal for his constant inspiration and encouragement to publish the project report in the form of a book.

I received all sorts of help and co-operation from Dr. T.K. Chatteerjee, former Registrar and Dr. D.K. Sarkar, the present Registrar, of the University of North Bengal, in connection with this research study and for which I am indebted to both of them. My sincere thanks are due to my collegues of the department of Sociology, Anthropology and Centre for Himalayan Studies, University of North Bengal, for their constructive comments on the subject under study.

I like to record my deep sense of gratitude to my teacher Sri Biswanath Bannerjee, Department of Anthropology, University of Calcutta, for his valuable suggestions in connection with this study.

Mr. Samsuddin Khan deserve special thanks and appreciation for his association and involvement with this research project as Field Assistant. He must be credited for assisting and conducting field study. The completion of this research would have been impossible without his thoughtful cooperation. Thanks are due to the *Jari* artisans of four villages among whom field work was conducted for the sake of this research. I am also thankful to my Research Scholars

Mr. Ganesh Chandra Mollick and Mr. Rajib Chatterjee for helping me in proof correction of the manuscript.

Finally, I wish to thank my wife Dr. Begum Rokaiya Kohinoor and my son Master Raunak Rony for their unfailing support and understanding to complete this research study and to publish it as a book.

I am conscious of limitations of this study. I therefore, welcome constructive comments and suggestions from the readers as an ethic of a researcher.

Prof. Sekh Rahim Mondal
North Bengal University Campus
Dist. Darjeeling, West Bengal
Pin-734430

1

Introduction

Industries in India

In India, industries can be categorised into three groups — large and medium scale industries, small scale industries and traditional rural or cottage industries. The first group is in a position to manage its business and enjoys access to technical knowledge, licenses, export avenues, road materials, and sheltered market net works. These industries are also able to arrange loans from financial institutions and commercial banks and to employ technical manpower. While industries comprising of the second and third groups have some specific features which require special attention. Small and rural/cottage industries face problems in upgradation of their techniques and technology, acquisition of tools, getting raw materials, obtaining finance from commercial banks, developing markets for their products and getting information regarding their products and trades.

Village and Small Industries : Nature and Scope :

The village or the rural industry can be defined as 'Any production or processing activity outside the farm - big or small, traditional or modern, organized or unorganized - which utilizes the resources endowment (man and materials) of a village or any other rural area'.

The village and rural industry sector is divided into eight sub-sectors, namely, khadi, village industries, handlooms, sericulture, handicrafts, coir, small scale industries and power looms. Among these sub-sectors, the first six constitute traditional industries and the last two represent modern small industries (Seventh Five Years Plan 1985-90).

Rural industries constitute an important segment of Indian economy. They provide employment next in size only to the agricultural sector and account for more than one-third of the total exports from India. This sector has preponderance of self-employment, resulting in wide dispersal of industrial and economic activities, ensuring maximum utilization of local resources, both man and material (Singh and Taori, 1993).

When agriculture functions as the heart of the Indian economy, rural industries act as lungs with interlinkages of the highest order between these two. The small village industries are largely functioning at the subsistence level of economy owing to : (a) inefficiency of the production methods used, (b) lack of co-operative production, (c) lack of institutional finance and raw materials, (d) limited market opportunities, (e) limited communication channels, (f) lack of awareness about strategies for promotion of products and (g) lack of facilities of skill improvement. However, in recent times some marginal changes have occurred in the pattern and organization of work and use of raw materials in the production activities of the traditional cottage industries. New tools and technology, organization of work, and utilization of raw materials, are considered as the main instruments for improving the efficiency of work. In recent times, impact of urbanization, particularly proximity to the urban areas and growth of communication, has facilitated availability of new tools and technologies. As a consequence, some improvements and changes have taken place in the production processes of rural and cottage industries. (Solunki, 1993).

Government Policies on Village and Small Industries (VSI) Sector :

The Government of India has always given priority to the village and small industries sector in its Industrial Policy Resolution and in the strategies for industrialzation. With de-regulation of Indian economy, a new package of policy measures for promoting and strengthening the VSI sector was announced on 6th August, 1991. These policy measures have given thrust to simplification of regulations and procedures, improvement of economic viability of these units, improvement of their competitive strength, export promotion, enhancement of credit flow to the sector, prompt payment of loans and development of integrated infrastructure for the sector. In the Industrial policy of 1991, 836 products were reserved for exclusive production in the small scale industry sector.

The 9th plan lays emphasis on improvement of VSI through the following measures :

(i) The small scale and village industries will be provided incentives and support to their growth and employment. It will be ensured that foreign investment does not displace such industries.

(ii) The list of items reserved for small scale industries (SSI) will be reviewed with a view to achieving benefits of economies of sale, technological upgradation, and improvement of export capabilities,

(iii) Credit flow to small .scale industries sector will be augmented and the financial institutions will be motivated to offer loans to SSI liberally.

(iv) The Khadi and village industries commission (KVIC) will be financially strengthened to be able to generate more opportunities under the '2 million jobs programme'.

(v) Technology development upgradation in the VSI sector, especially in the case of small scale industries, handlooms, powerlooms, coir, handicrafts, wool etc. will receive special attention.

(vi) For the improvement of economic and working conditions of workers in the unorganized sector, a muiltidimensional approach will be adopted with involvement of voluntary organizations

(NGO). Schemes will be launched for the welfare of persons engaged in the unorganized sector and for bringing about awareness among them about their legislative entitlement. (Nineth Five Year Plan 1997-2002).

Capital Structure of Small Scale and Village Industries :

The capital requirements of small units depend on their size and the manufacturing processes involved in them. Besides the local moneylenders, relatives and brothers-in-profession are the main sources of funds for the small scale village industries. Institutional financial assistance are rather very scanty. Thus the small units almost always experience shortage of finance. Banks and other financial institutions provide loan only to reputed and organized sectors. The village and small unorganized sectors facing difficulties in fulfilling the conditions laid down by financial institutions and commercial banks.

Financial crisis or lack of capital is the major obstacle for growth of the small and village industry in the country. In this sector, there is no sufficient profit which can sustain its growth. The financial assistance provided by the Government is also insufficient. If adequate and timely financial support at low rates of interest is provided to small and village industries, they will be able to make use of modern tools and implements for effective diversification in their production. This will also lead to socio-economic development of the workers or artisans, besides providing employment to a large number of people.

Prospect of Small Scale and Village Industries in India :

In India we find small and village industries almost in all places. These industries have a great scope and potential for development in view of their unique features and inherent qualities of products which have helped to keep the traditional heritage and artistic beauty of the products. Small and village industries require low capital investment and provides employment opportunities to rural masses. The local and outside markets for these industrial products are available round the year. The small industries sector accounting for 8.5 percent of the fixed capital, was employing nearly 50 per cent of the total workers, whereas, large factories accounting for a share of 43 per cent in total fixed capital employed only 7 per cent of the total workers (Sinha, 1990)

The small and village industries have tremendous scope for development. Introduction of modern designs of articles can surely pave the way for speedy progress of rural crafts Diversification in products could save them from the danger posed to their crafts by big industries. What is required is a well-planned strategy to impress upon the entrepreneurs about the urgency to acquire knowledge about production of modern articles and items which have a ready wider market. For this, various facilities have to be offered to them. Publicity campaigns need to be lanched to create awareness and educate people about their crafts. Simultaneously, their skills ought to be sharpened, so that they can undertake the production of various utility articles which are in demand. Training facilities at the door steps of small and village industries are required to give a fillip to this sector.

Growth of Village and Small Industries :

There is lack of reliable data on village and small industries sector, particularly on traditional group of industries. A broad picture that emerges in terms of production, export and employment is given in table 1.1.

Table 1.1

Changes in Status of Village and Small Industries in Recent Year

Years	1984 - 85		1989-90			1996-97		
Types of Industries	TI	SSI	TI	SSI	% Increase	TI	SSI	% Increase
Production (Rs.in million)	772563	569430	123690	1019450	73	414320	2533430	158
Export (Rs.in million)	22070	23500	71809.8	76260	247	300150	20200	239
Employment (in million)	16.49	12.20	22.05	16.40	22	32.82	22.55	44

Notes : Tl - Traditional Industries, SSI - Small Scale Industries
(Source : 7th and 8th Five Year Plans, Government of India).

Performance of VSI Sector :

The rate of growth of village and small industries during the first few years of the eurrent decade was slow, but it picked up at later stage. The statistics indicating the performance of the small scale industries are given in Table 1.2.

Table 1.2

Performance of Small Scale Industries in Recent Year

Years	Production at current price Level (Rs.in million)	Employment (In million)	Exports (Rs.in million)	No. of small scale Industrial Units (In million)
1991-92	1786990	12.98	138830	2.08
1992-93	2093000	13.46	177840	2.25
1993-94	2416480	13.94	253070	2.38
1994-95	2939900	14.66	264000	2.57

(*Source*: Annual Report, Small Scale Industries, Ministry of Industry, 1995-96).

Economic Reforms vis-a-vis Small and Village Industries :

Uplift of the rural economy as a whole can not become viable and sustainable unless industry and more specifically heavy industry, grows at a rate faster than the other segments of economy, including agriculture. The rural industries with their age old technologies were exporting about 30 per cent of their products, but for various reasons these slowly started backsteping with little exposure at outside resulting into an almost stagnant situation.

Unfortunately, libcralization has misled some people into believing that self-reliance has no relevance ! In fact, at one time, the confederation of the Indian Industry suggested elimination of all restrictions on technology imports and foreign collaboration. But for reasons the removal of restrictions was not 100 per cent and under such a situation considerable liberalization indeed taken place. Since the adoption of new Industrial policy (1991), approvals by the Reserve Bank for technology imports are allowed in cases pertaining to specific industries. This allow the small and rural industries to propagate and flourish further.

For the growth of industrial sector, initially proper thrust was not given to integration of large and small industries. This resulting to an initial setback in rural industries. But soon government realized the situation steps were taken to strengthen the programmes of ancillarization to establish and improve linkages between large and small industries, leading to harmonious growth of the industrial sector. In addition, rural industries are generally exposed to improved technology, wider market net work and all these gradually overcome the initial setback.

Small Industries and Child Labour :

Various estimates reveal that the problem of child labour has been growing in India. UNESCO reported that, India possesses the significant number of child labours in the globe. 1981 census puts the figure at 13.64 million, 1991 census puts it at 14.5 million, 1993 National Sample Survey puts it at 17.3 million. An estimate of child workers in India from 1981-2000 A.D. is presented in Table 1.3.

Table 1.3

Projection of Child Workers in India : 1981 to 2000 A.D.

Year	Child Labour (5-14 years) in Million
1981	13.64
1983	17.36
1985	17.58
1990	18.17
2000	20.15

(*Source* : The table is abstracted from Triparthy : 1997).

The magnitudes of the problem of child labour varies from rural to urban areas and also from male to female child workers. It is a generalized fact that the rate of child labourer in rural areas is much more higher than the urban areas. However, in urban areas too the children work for long hours. Further, the number of child labour varies from organized sector to unorganized sector. In unorganized sector child labour exists in a greater extent due to the very nature of works. In the country there are innumerable child labourers in small and rural home based industries. For the need of family and survival many children are found to be frequently working in small and village industries. As the child labourers are not organized on the lines of trade unions, thus they cannot fight for their rights and interests. The embroidery or *jari* work with which present research has been focused is a labour intensive small industry where involvement of child labour is very much noticed.

What is a Child ?

Different laws have set varying age limits for the determination of what is a child. As per ILO convention No. 138, in conjunction with "labour" the general limit of age of a child is 15 years or under special national circumstances, 14 years (Fyfe, 1993).

According to Indian Constitution child is a person who has not completed his or her 15 years of age (Legislation of India : 1979). According to Child Labour Protection and Regulation Act, 1986, child means a persons who has completed his or her 14 years of age.

What is Child Labour ?

This is child in work which is exploitative, and threatens the health, welfare and development of children.

In the context of child labour, a working defination of a "child" may be a person below the general limit of 15 years or in special circumstances 14 years, set by ILO minimum age convention 1973 (No. 138).

Child labour considered to be an exploitation as the children : (a) work at too young age, (b) work too long hours, (c) work for too little pay, (d) work in hazardous conditions, (e) work under slave like arrangement.

It is commonly believed that child labour is the work done by children who are in the age group of 4-14 years, paid or unpaid, and remain busy for many hours of the day within or outside the family. (Fyfe, 1993).

Approaches to Child Labour :

A comprehensive strategy has been adopted by ILO to eliminate child labour which are to be operated at four levels of society, viz. the child, the family, the community and the Government. It will involve at least five types of intervention, viz. education and training, welfare services, protected work, advocacy, regulation and enforcement.

Education and training considered as the singlemost important remedy to child labour problem. But payments must be able to afford this and of course schooling must be made available. (Fyfe, 1993).

The Study of Traditional Arts and Crafts :

In order to retain the relevance of the fast changing world, the social scientific researches have started by playing a new role in the protection and conservation of cultural diversity and documentation of indigenous knowledge system, which go hand in hand. The traditional knowledge bases of the communities, specially the skills of indigenous arts and crafts of the world over are now being threatened and eroded by the growing tide of modern mechanized technification and homogenization of the planet. Modern development strategy has taken the form of mega projects which is going to destroy the indigenous knowledge system relating to habits, arts and crafts of the indigenous traditional communities. Such destruction may drag mankind towards gradual disaster. Under such a situation protection of cultural diversity as well as artistic heritage of indigenous communities is very much necessary both for economic as well as for socio-cultural significance.

The protection of cultural diversity as well as the artistic heritage shall come from scientific study of the validity of plurality and complexity of indigenous knowledge system which have grown under specific socio-historico-cultural circumstances. The study have to demonstrate that similarity of cultural heritage among communities may due to common source of origin or cultural borrowing or parallel and coordinate developments following from similar needs and contexts. The traits of culture like that of artistic skills, classical or folk, great or little, written or oral traditions should be examined from the nature and nature specific to temporal and spatial contexts.

The social scientific researches have to play a role in exhibiting, protecting and documenting cultural diversity against unsustainable development and unauthorized extraction of cultural and human resources. In order to fulfil this goal, the social scientists have taken the role to help the communities to codify, classify, analyse and communicate their cultural/artistic data in their own form, explore and strengthen the indigenous knowledge systems, customs, myths and rituals which help them to cultivate their artistic habits and skills to live in harmony with the social and natural environment. The scientific enquiry of indigenous habits and cultural landscapes may help to integrate the diversity of cultural heritage with socio-economic activities of the communities in a dynamic spatial continuum. The elements of heritage could be harnessed to compatible uses involving community participation.

The researchers of traditional arts and crafts today have to reconsider their roles of collecting, documenting, analysing and exhibiting the artifacts and art objects as specimens of vanishing cultures or of documenting the irreversible progress of technological civilization. But they must collaborate with the communities and artists in their cultural recuperation and self determination. With this change in role, social scientists no longer be treated by communities/artists as analysts of cultural diversity and knowledge, but as partners in the struggle for their restitution and preservation of knowledge and skill.

The social science researches on Indian culture and civilization have to be focused into two broad contexts : (a) material art of life and (b) socio-religious life. The traditional arts and crafts belonging to the former; while the social organization, believes and customs consisting of the later. The recording and analysing of indigenous knowledge system relating to those contexts are very much necessary under the present changing situation.

Traditional arts and crafts have been the very breath of Indian civilization since time immemorial. The continuation of these traditional skills are not only the nations pride but have significant contribution in the economic well being of the people and civilization of the country. Since agriculture and large scale mechanised industries failed to provide full employment in the country, so a section of less privileged people in rural and urban sectors have to resort to various kinds of self-employment activities for their survival which includes their involvement in marginally lucrative cottage industries like ari work, *jari* work and various other craft working. The production of traditional arts and crafts and their entire production system is guided essentially by verbal testimonies, this fall under the category of little tradition i.e. *laukik* or *desi* culture. Research studies on traditional craft works are rather very meagre. But such studies are very essential not only for their documentation and examination, but also for economic and cultural significance of the crafts under contemporary changing situation.

II

The Background of the Study :

In India hand embroidery or *jari* work is an important unorganized sector of artistic production. It is one such cottage or home industry which has long tradition and a greater role in Indian economy, culture and civilization. *jari* work is considered as one of the best traditional artistic craft of this country. Designing through guilded threads and coloured materials is the basic artistic theme of embroidary work. Golden or silver thread *i.e. jari* or *ari* which is the basic material with which embroiders work for designing the cloths has a special meaning and significance to the Indian people.

The history evident that embroidery worked dress materials of exquisite beauty were manufactured by Indian craftsmen since very past. Thus embroidery has continued to be inextricably connected with the Indian culture. Originally this artistic craft was developed at West Asia and later propagated at northern parts of India during the medieval era. Subsequently the craft spread at various pockets of the country, specially at Muslim inhabited areas of the places like Lucknow, Surat, Bombay, Delhi and Calcutta.

There are many places in Bengal, such as the city of Calcutta and its associated rural hinterlands where embroidery or *jari* work played an important role in economic life or the inhabitants. Most probably embroidery work once started at Bengal in some places of Calcutta and later spread over at nearby villages of the districts of Howrah. In Howrah district *the jari* work is widely prevalent among the Muslims of the places like Panchla, Korola, Domjur, Bauria and Uluberia. Now a days the *jari* work is the most flourishing small scale industrial enterprise of these places.

It is reported that nearly seventy percent of Muslim households living in and around the above localities are engaged in *jari* work for their livelihood. Many scheduled caste people of the said areas are also associated with this craft for their sustenance. The *jari* work is done by both men and women belonging to Muslim and Hindu communities. For various reasons the ongoing closure of large scale factory industries at Howrah industrial belt resulting into a mass unemployment. Under such a context they *jari* work has provided an opportunity to many of the unemployed labours either to involve personally or to engage their sons and daughters to work with this craft for their livelihood.

Statement of the Problem :

The craft of embroidery has both economic and cultural relevance. The embroidery work has provided employment opportunities to many and at the same time embroidery worked dress material has a good demand in domestic and international markets. In India the biggest market of this craft is northern and western parts of the country. There has been a great demand of this craft in foreign markets like Central and West Asia, Africa, and various parts of South and South East Asia. The garments as well as other cloth items with embroidery works are very much favourite to women irrespective of their religious and cultural identities. During marriage and other social occasions embroidery worked dress materials are of special significance.

The manufacturing of *jari* work is either done in small workshops or in households. As per conventional system, bare cloths are supplied by traders *(mahajans)* of the city to the master artisans *(ustagar)* and the designing of embroider) is done by the workers *(majur)*. Finally, the finished product passes through one or two levels of middle men in the villages until it reaches to the *mahajans* again. Actually the whole industry of *jari* embroidery is being regulated and controlled by the *mahajans*. As the marketing of this craft is exclusively controlled by the *mahajans* their profit is quite high. While the profit of the *ustagar* is quite lucrative as they regulate the entire production system. But the earning of the *majurs* is much low as there is no fixed wage rate for the artisans. The demand of this craft is highly seasonal so the artisans (workers) entirely depend upon the *Ustagars* as well as *muhajans* for the sake of their artistic work.

The *jari* artisans are unorganized. Their social position is somewhat low in village society. *Jari* work is mainly done by Muslim boys. At times girls too participate in this work. The artisans are mainly coming from poor families who work mostly on contractual basis. The artisans of *jari* work are mainly the child labourers. The artistic skill of hand embroidery has some adverse effects on health and eye sight of the artisans. Involvement of child labour, low income and seasonality of work creates a psychological tension and sense of insecurity among the *jari* artisans.

Considering the situation of unemployment in our country and socio-cultural significance of this craft, it is necessary to preserve and encourage the embroidery industry. To avoid the ill effects of this craft production there is a need to modernize the technology of this industry. Finally, development programmes are also needed to help the artisans for the sake of their socio-economic development.

Considering the above facts the study of hand embroidery (*jari* work) as a traditional Indian craft and the embroiders (*jari* artisans) as an occupational group is very much necessary. As a part of this endeavour the aspects of technology, work organization and economy of this craft as well as the social life of the artisans have to be examined and analysed for the sake of documentation and also for necessary intervention. But unfortunately anthropologists, sociologist and other social scientists have not paid much attention to study this craft and the craft makers. But such study is essential both for academic as well as for practical purposes.

Studies on Embroidery (*Jari*) Work :

The research work on hand embroidery *or jari* work is rather very scanty. In the field of anthropological and sociological researches on *jari* work in India mention can be made of the following works.

Begum *(1995)* examined how the marginal section of rural poor, specially the women, have to subsist on the less lucrative cottage industries like *jari* work in rural areas of the district of Howrah in West Bengal. The impact of *jari* industry on life of the artisans was also highlighted by her. She observed that less profitable craft works persist among the marginal section of the village community and continue to be held by them because of their position in social ladder. She noted that the *jari* work is practiced by women of marginal class as a last resort to their survival and is exploited by the businessmen to a maximum extent. The study suggest that the problem require special attention from the Government and the agencies of social welfare who should come to rescue these least organized craftsmen and ensure better return for their future.

Kumar (1988) conducted a'study among *the jari* workers of some villages of the district of Howrah and suggested strategies for improving their income levels. In his study he also highlighted on three major aspects of this craft work like manufacturing, input and marketing.

Manna (1994) wrote an article on *jari* embroidery of a village in West Bengal. In this article he has presented a profile of *the Jari* embroiders including their nature and organization of works. The problems of this craft and craftmakers were also discussed by him.

Mondal (1979) studied the *jari* work in a Muslim village of West Bengal. His study reveals the technology of *Jari* industry, its employer-employee relations, the consumers of the craft and its social significance among the people. The socio-cultural life of the *jari*-artisans was also examined by him. The author observed that they *jari* work has both positive and negative effects among its workers. He suggested that co-operative and banking facilities to be offered to the poor artisans by which they can afford to prerserve and use their skills better. In this context he also recommended that the ill effects of *jari* work can be avoided by undertaking development programmes for the artisans. In his recent studies, Mandal (2006a, 2006b) thoroughly examined the entrepreneurial behaviour of the *jari* embroiders as well as the empowerment issues of the women artisans engaged in *jari* embroidery.

The review of above works clearly suggest the fact that the studies on *jari* work are practically very negligible. Thus it deserves immediate attention to study this craft and the craft makers as well as the entrepreneurs at empirical context. Therefore, an intensive study on the craft of *jari* embroidery and the embroiders has been taken into consideration.

Aims and Objectives :

The basic aims of this research is to conduct a detailed and indepth study on social framework of hand embroidery (*jari* work) with an intention to suggest strategies for developing this craft and also to improve the quality of life of the artisans. With the above aims in mind the objectives of this research is to enquire and highlight the following aspects :

(1) To find out the manufacturing process (tools and technology) of the craft and the division of labour involved in this craft production.

(2) To examine the employer-employee relations in the context of manufacturing of this craft.

(3) To analyse the entrepreneural activities and the system of its marketing.

(4) To examine the structure and organization of this small scaled home industry.

(5) To find out the price and profit margin of the traders, middlemen and craftmakers.

(6) To highlight the economic, social and cultural significance of this craft in contemporary changing situation.

(7) To enquire the social background of entrepreneurs and the craftmakers.

(8) To examine the economic, social and cultural life of the *jari* embroiders.

(9) To find out the effect of *jari* work in village society and to highlight the nature, extent and problems of child labour involved in *jari* work.

(10) To examine the problems and to explore the prospects of *jari* industry.

To substantiate the above objectives the study has been planned to present a profile of *jari* industry covering the following aspects :

(i) The emergence and the growth of this craft in India.

(ii) The technology as well as the system of production of this craft.

(iii) The work and the work organization of this craft production.

(iv) The employer-employee relations.

(v) The social background of the craftmakers and their style of life.

(vi) The impact of *jari* work on the life of the artisans as well as on the village society.

(vii) The *jari* work and the involvement of child labour.

(viii) The problems as well as the prospects of this artistic craft under present situation.

The purpose of this study is of three folds. Firstly, it will help us in documentation of technology of this traditional artistic craft. Secondly, the study shall explore and highlight the problems of the craft and the craft producers. Finally, the result of the study shall help to evolve some strategies for growth of this craft and development of the craftmakers.

III

Methodology

Research Design :

The design for the proposed research has been formulated on the basis of aims and objectives of the study. The locale of study, the subject of enquiry, and the tools and techniques of data collection are all related with the nature of the study. The main purpose of this study is to gain an insight and experience on social framework of a traditional craft as well as its problems and prospects. This is an exploratory study with diagnostic outlook wherever necessary. The approach of this research is structure-functional. For this research both qualitative and quantitative data have been used. The facts are presented through descriptive as well as analytical manners. The comparative method, both synchronic and diachronic over space (place) and time (generations) have been adopted for understanding the present situation of this craft and the changes those have taken place in it from past to present context. The research was conducted in a wholistic manner.

There are three major areas in which this study was conducted. These are (a) the manufacturing process of the craft and its marketing process; (b) the socio-economic life of the craftmakers; and (c) the nature, extent and problems of child labour involved in this craft production.

The existing situation of *jari* work and the associated matters to this craft have been examined. These are recorded here for the sake of documentation since no serious study was conducted on the said subject. By examining the various aspects of *jari* work some problems of this artistic craft have been identified. On the basis of empirical findings various solutions have also been formulated.

To understand the manufacturing operation of this artistic craft and the life of the artisans, field study was conducted in four villages of the district of Howrah in West Bengal. The *jari* workshop *(karkhand)* and individual families those involved in *jari* work in the villages were studied for the purpose. To understand the manufacturing process data were collected on use of raw materials, techniques of embroidery, nature and type of works done, division of labour, organization of work, number of persons and manpower involved to complete a work, quality and quantity of production of the craft per month and the wage rate of the artisans. To get an idea about trading and marketing process of this craft a survey was also conducted at Barabazar market of Kolkata. The data were gathered in this context consisting of traders-suppliers relations, entrepreneural activities, terms of production, nature of demand and supply, items of clothing and nature of design, the price range and profit margin of the suppliers and the traders etc. While for knowing the socio-economic life of the artisans an intensive study was also conduced among the artisans of different villages. The aspects which have been taken into consideration are : age, sex, family background, knowledge of skill, experience, economic status, income, education, interpersonal relation, organizational behaviour, political participation, religious habit, dress, food, housetype, leisure, recreation, health culture, aspiration, problem and frustration. Emphasis has also been given to highlight how the artisan's (child artisan's) work requirement have affected their family life and personality development.

Locales of the Study

In this study I have tried to present a profile of *jari* embroidery as a craft and the embroiders as an artisan group. As a part of that endeavour, I have dealt on the various facets of the technology and economies of the craft and the socio-economic life of the craft makers. I have for several months studied the embroiders at work, mixed with them, and ascertained their attitudes to different social and cultural issues.

As it is a detailed enquiry on a traditional craft and the craft makers so the research was conducted in places where the artistic skill of *jari* embroidery is prevalent among a group of the people since very past. Owing to certain structural limitations, a total of four villages were selected for field study. While selecting the villages the concentration of *jari* artisans in them and the types of *jari* work done by the artisans including historical depth of this artistic craft at the places were taken into consideration.

For this research four artisan villages of the district of Howrah were selected from the police stations of Damjur, Sankrail, Panchla and Bauria. The name of the villages are Dakshin Korola, Uttar Dhulagori, Sahapur and Paschim Bauria respectively. The villages were selected purposively considering the concentration of *jari* artisans in them and their nature of craft production. The villages as well as the places selected for this study have some special significance as they are regarded as very important pockets of *jari* work not only of the district of Howrah, but also of whole West Bengal since very beginning. It is also to be noted here that the said localities are very famous and having national and international reputation for *jari* embroider).

Data Collection

The data for this study was collected both from secondary as well as from primary sources. For getting background information various published and unpublished news, reports and documentary materials relating to *jari* work were consulted and reviewed. While the primary data was collected through intensive field studies among the *jari* artisans of four villages. The empirical field studies were conducted in a planned manner as per needs of this research.

Selection of Informants

To obtain necessary and relevant information at field situation the informants were selected from all the four villages. The informants were chosen from artisan families who were directly involved with the craft of *jari* embroidery. To select the informants it was decided to depend on their sincerity and reliability of providing correct information, appreciation of questions they were asked to answer and their capability to provide the proper and correct facts. Since *jari* work is done by both men and women artisans, so the informants were both males as well as females. Selected informants were of two types, viz.

key informants and occasional helpers. The help of key informants were taken for furnishing most of the data on the basis of set of questions framed for this study. While occasional helpers were the expert and busy artisans or the entrepreneurs of *jari* work the help of whom were taken for verification of collected data and also for obtaining some additional information.

Tools, Techniques and Methods of Data Collection

The data for this research were collected with the help of standard anthropological tools and techniques. At the initial stage pilot survey was conducted in different villages of the district of Howrah to identify the villages where *jari* work has been practiced by the artisans at a large number. On the basis of concentration of artisan households, four villages were selected for field study. At the second stage it was planned to collect indepth data through intensive field study among the artisans (*jari* workers) of each of the selected village to understand the manufacturing operations (work, work organization and working relations) of this craft and socio-economic life of the craftmakers. Specific data were collected with the help of schedules. Three sets of schedule were constructed for this study. Schedule 'A' was used for the study of embroiders, schedule "B' used for the study of *jari* workshop, and schedule "C" was used for the study of suppliers and sellers.

The schedules were by and large consisted of close ended questions, although there were certain open ended questions too. Close ended questions were designed to get objective data about social background and social situation of the *jari* artisans. While the open ended questions were aimed at asking the informants to explain their own views about their activities and problems relating to *jari* work. Most of the data were gathered with the help of schedules. The information gathered from the informants through schedules was further supplemented by free dialogue with them. Some useful suggestion and information given by the informants were also incorporated. Schedules were prepared on the basis of pre-testing through pilot study.

In addition to the use of schedules, intensive study was also conduced in the four villages through depth interview, key informant's interview, case study, group discussion and observation. Necessary photographs were also taken for the sake of documentation.

It was stated that there are three major areas to which this study has been focused. The existing system of manufacturing operations, the socio-economic life of the artisans, the input and the output as well as the marketing system of *jari* products have been examined here. These are studied since there was no proper record on this craft and no scientific study was conducted at past. It is planned that by analysing and evaluating the existing system some alternative proposals shall be formulated.

For knowing the manufacturing operation the *jari* workshops as well as the individual families working in their home were studied. While for knowing the socio-economic life of the artisans study was conducted among the different categories of *jari* embroiders. Altogether 147 artisans were studied. The villages surveyed for this purpose were Korola, Dhulagori, Sahapur and Rameswarbati. Finally, to get the information on trading system of this artistic craft a study was also conducted among the suppliers and traders. Calcutta market was also visited to understand the trading system specially the demand and supply of the *jari* products.

Data Processing and Analysis :

The data gathered for this study were processed after necessary checking and editing. In course of processing the completeness and accuracy of data was looked carefully The field data collected through schedules were analysed systematically.

Tabulation was done manually. Data were analysed quantitatively and qualitatively. Simple statistical methods comprising mainly of percentages were calculated. No further statistical analysis was incorporated. Since study has a comparative perspective some cross tabulations have also been presented. The qualitative data obtained through interviews, case studies, group discussion and observation were presented through systematic description of the facts with analytical perspective. In course of analysis methods of comparison was also adopted. The data were finally organized into relevant chapters.

Presentation of Data and Contents:

The material of the study has been presented into 11 chapters. Chapter 1 is the Introduction which outlines the statement of problems, aims and objective and methodology. Chapter 2 is on *Jari* Embroidery Works in Bengal. Chapter 3 is the Technology of *Jari* Embroidery. Chapter 4 is on Structure and Organization of Production. Chapter 5 is on The Entrepreneurs and the Enterprise. Chapter 6 is dealing with The Economic aspects of *jari* Craft. Chapter 7 is Socio-Economic Profile of the *jari* Artisans of Four Villages. Chapter 8 is devoted for an account of Women *jari* Embroiders and Empowerment. Chapter 9 is the highlights on Embroidery Works and The Child Labour. Chapter 10 is Portraits of *jari* Embroiders. Chapter 11 is Embroidery works and Embroiders — Problems, Prospects and Priorities which recapitulates the main findings and implications of this study. Some policy prescriptions are also stated in this section. The tables are presented in relevant chapters.

Limitations of the Present Study :

The study has certain limitations. Since the empirical study on "The Embroidery works and the Embroiders in Bengal" has been undertaken for the first time purely on academic angle, so the benefits of earlier research were not available. Hence as a exploratory study this research has its own limitations. Secondly, the study was conducted only on four villages of the district of Howrah in West Bengal, hence the observations drawn from this research cannot be generalized too for covering the features of the craft and craftmakers of whole of India. However, the findings of the study provide broad clues about the craft and the craftsmen not only of the state of West Bengal, but also of other places. It is assumed that the operations in other places also follow a similar pattern. The purpose of the study shall be fulfilled more if similar studies shall undertake in future with large sample at other places of the country where the similar craft is produced by the craftsmen.

The data for this study, particularly of economic aspects and marketing of the craft were collected on the basis of survey. This may not be completely correct since vested interest of the middlemen and traders were involved. This is exclusively true for peofit margin of the entrepreneurs and businessmen of this craft. One of the biggest limitation of this study is the non-consideration of market net works of this craft business, hence a detailed study on this aspect is also very much needed in future.

2

Jari Emboridery Works in Bengal

History of *Jari* Embroidery in India :

The *jari* work is a hand embroidery using gold and silver coloured metalic wires and other designing materials. The artistic craft of *jari* embroidery is said to be originated first at middle-east, specially in Iran, where some centuries ago a saint, named Yusuf Ali Salam invented and introduced this craft. The word *jari* has come from Iranian word *jardoji,* which means "gold wire'. From Iran the craft of *jari* embroidery was brought to India by some professional artisans to cater the needs, of medieval Royal families. In India *jari* embroidery flourished much under the patronage of Mughal rulers. Actually, the Muslim rulers (Badshas and Nawabs) did a lot for the growth and development of this craft in India. Subsequently, the craft of *jari* embroidery spread all over the country, particularly in Muslim inhabited areas of the states of Uttar Pradesh, Rajasthan, Gujrat, Delhi, Maharashtra, Behar and West Bengal. The embroidery worked dress materials was basically liked by the Muslim and non-Muslim aristocrats owing to their artistic beauty and gorgeous nature. Gradually, this craft attracted the attention of middle class as well the common masses of all communities.

Jari Embroidery in Bengal:

Jari embroidery is one of the traditional artistic crafts of India which has flourished in Bengal during recent past. Golden thread *(Kasap)* which is the basic material with which the embroiders *(karigurs)* work has a special meaning for Bengal and Bengalis. The art of *jari* embroidery was initially developed at northern and western parts of India, later propagated and nourished in Bengal for various reasons. The city of Surat (Sourastra) is considered to be the centre of production of *jari* threads and other *jari* materials necessary for embroidery works. In Bengal these materials are available in Calcutta market.

There are many places in Bengal such as Calcutta, and Howrah the names of them leave no doubt that the *jari* embroidery plays an important role in the economic life of many people living in those places. Most probably, *jari* embroidery was flourished as a cottage industry in some areas of Calcutta and some villages of the district of Howrah and then propagated in other places of Bengal.

The original *jari* embroiders of Bengal were divided into two major works of activities, i.e., Aari-work *(Aarir kaj)* and *Jari* work *(Jarir kaj)*. The embroiders were organized on the basis of their specialized guilds. The main centre of embroidery works shifted with time from one place to another. Initially the *jari* work was started by the Muslim artisans, but in course of time, people of various other communities as well as castes accepted the art of embroidery as their profession. Thus among the *jari* embroiders there are Muslims as well as Hindus and others. Actually, the Muslim artisans are traditionally associated with the art of *jari* embroidery, but later a number of Hindus also took this profession. Gradually, embroiders of particular localities specialized in specific branch of embroidery, and some areas won a reputation for a particular type of work. At present there are several thousand of good embroiders living in different villages of the district of Howrah. Embroidery work at a large scale is localized in certain areas of Calcutta and Howrah. In Calcutta the most important centre of *jari* works are Barabazar, Rajabazar, Matiabruj etc. While in the district of Howrah the important centres of production are Dhulagori, Korola, Latibpur, Panchla and Bauria. The embroiders of different places of West Bengal like Calcutta and mofusil areas of Howrah are noted for expertise in different branches of *jari* embroidery. For example there are villages in the police stations of Howrah district like Damjur, Sankrail, Panchla and Bauria which are nationally and internationally famous for varieties of *jari* works. The embroiders of the villages like Dhulagori. Korola, Kushodanga, Gabbaria, Bonharishpur, Latibpur, Panchla, Khajuri, Paschim Bauria, and Raghudebbati are well recognized as the important places for classical experts of the art of *jari* embroidery. Nearly 85 percent of the people of those villages are directly or indirectly associated with the *jari* works. Though some particular places in Bengal are reputed for *jari* embroidery yet the craft is not confined to those places only. In many villages of

Bengal those are situated nearer to Calcutta there are artisans who are involved with this craft production.

The embroider group of Bengal occupies a distinct place in social life. Bengali women irrespective of castes and communities like women of other parts of India, are fond of embroidery worked dress materials. However, the taste of Bengali women are little bit different from that of women in other provinces. And this Bengali taste, rooted in traditional Bengali culture, manifests itself, among other things, in the preference for certain patterns and designs of embroidery. Many of these preferred designs are drawn from familiar objects of Bengal flora and fauna. Bengal has a distinct 'school of embroidery', with motifs drawn from traditional folk art. However, an aristocratic touch has been followed. Without the artistic work done by the Bengali embroiders, the Bengal culture would, clearly be impoverished and economic as well as social life in Bengal would definitely lose much of its glitter and gloss.

The embroiders' work may not be an essential to the economic existence of the people of Bengal as the work of other artisans, but it is, nonetheless, an important artistic craft of this province. Without having embroidery worked dress items, specially in ceremonial occasions, the women, particularly middle class urban women's world be a void. It is impossible to think of a wedding in an Indian as well as a Bengali rich and upper middle class family without thinking of a set of embroidery worked *sari* or other dress items for the bride. Embroidery worked garments and clothings are merely articles of luxury, but customs and traditions transformed them into almost a conventional necessity in welltodo families of Bengal and of the whole country. The embroiders who produce this necessity have, thus, become an important component of Indian social structure.

In West Bengal *jari* work is being done in different pockets of south-eastern parts of the state since long back. But the district of Howrah is probably the oldest and largest centre of *jari* designers of this state. The *jari* artisans of Bengal are considered as the best for production of this craft throughout the country. In the district of Howrah the *jari* work is widely prevalent in Domjur, Sankrail, Panchla, Bauria and Ulubaria police stations. The village Korola which is situated in the Sankrail police station is considered to be the oldest centre of this craft production in the district of Howrah. A pilot survey on *jari* work reveal that, nearly 85 percent of Muslim households living in villages of Sankrail, Panchla and Bauria police stations are directly or indirectly involved in *jari* work as means of their livelihood.

FINDINGS

The artistic craft of *jari* work is said to be originated first at Iran and later spread at western, northern and eastern parts of India under the patronage of medieval Muslim rulers. Earlier this artistic craft was basically produced by the Muslim artisans and used by the Muslim and non-Muslim aristocrats. But today both Muslim and non-Muslim artisans are involved with this craft production and it is gaining popularity among the common masses, both in the country as well as at abroad. In recent times *jari* work is prevalent in various parts of India specially in Rajasthan, Surat, Delhi, Bombay, Calcutta and its associated hinterlands. The district of Howrah in West Bengal is considered to be the largest centre of best *jari* designers in India. The most important places in the district of Howrah where *jari* work is being done today at a large scale are Dhulagori, Korola, Kushodanga, Gabbaria, Latibpur, Nalpur, Panchla, and Paschim Bauria.

3

The Technology of *Jari* Embroidery

The *jari* embroiders of different parts of India employ almost the same techniques for production of the craft. Another striking feature is that the techniques of *jari* work which was followed initially has been continuing till today. However, there are differences in motifs of the art of designing which varies from place to place. An attempt has been made here to present an outline of the main processes involved in this craft production. The *jari* work on dress items is being done both in small workshops called *karkhana* and also in the individual households called *ghar*. Thus the data on manufacturing process were gathered both from the workshops and also from households.

Materials and Tools Used :

The *jari* work is a hand embroidery. It is so named as the artisan.s using gold coloured metallic thread and other designing materials for producing this craft. The most important raw-materials and tools used by the artisans for production of their craft are as follows.

The materials used for this craft preparation are *kasap* (kala-pattu), golden *tiki, resumdauri, sifandouri, builen, dobka, chair, kanch, solma, moti, pipe, patthar, kutri, makhmal, tissue, gulli* etc. Normally the gold and silver *jari* threads as well as other materials of *jari* embroidery are produced at Surat of Saurashtra and these are procured by the local artisans from the Barabazar market of Calcutta (now Kolkata).

The most common tools used for this craft work are *Khoka, adda* or *dhadda* or *sumsera, arir-such* (needle), *kaichi* (scissor), *file* and tracing paper. For *jari* work usually a rectangular wooden frame is prepared by setting four wooden bars length and breadth wise, known as *adda* or *dhadda.* This rectangular frame is then placed over the four wooden stands called *khoka.* After attaching and placing the frame, the borders of the cloth to be embroidered are being set with the frame. The setting is done by stitching the sides of the cloth with attached tape of the frame known as *nefa.* The designs are then drawn on the piece of cloth for decoration with the artistic skills of hard embroidery. *Jari* embroidery involves a complicated work activity to which participation of skilled artisans, adults and children are very significant. These artisans are actually the embroiders. The craft of *jari* work requires drawing of designs on the piece of cloth for decoration with the designing objects through artistic skills of hand embroidery.

Techniques and Process of *Jari* Work :

The first stage *of jari* work comprises spreading of cloth lengthwise and fixing it strongly inside a rectangular frame called *adda*. The wooden frame is prepared by the local carpenters by setting four wooden bars length ($10^1/_2$' to 11') and breadth ($5^1/_2$' to 6') wise which are commonly known as *dhadda* and *samsera* respectively. The four corners of the wooden frame (*dhadda*) is then placed over the four wooden poles or stands, known as *khoka,* which is of a height of about $1^1/_2$' for placing the frame to remain fixed in a definite position necessary for *jari* work. After attaching and placing the frame, the cloth which is to be embroidered is being set with the frame. Setting is done by stitching the sides of the cloth with attached tape of the frame known as *nefa.* The designs are then drawn on the piece of cloth for decoration.

The only instrument that the artisans (*jari* embroiders) use is a small needle, inserted into a hollow piece of wood. These needles are not available in market. The *jari* workers procure big needles from the local markets and they themselves break each one of them into a few pieces. Each one of the broken pieces is converted into the special needle by filing. This special needle is popularly known as *arir such* or *jarir such.* Each needle is slightly bent at the lower end and giving it a shape like that of a hook so as to pull the *jari* thread from underneath the cloth.

At the second stage pictures, geometric figures are made on a wax paper and then impression is taken on the cloth on which *jari* work is to be done. The entire process of designing the border of figures and pictures is known as "*ari*". The raw materials used for designing are *kasap, builen, dobka, tiki, moti, douri, chir, kanch, solma* etc. The designed portion is now gently pressed by a wooden hammer which is flattened and smooth at the top. This helps in spreading of *jari* design evenly and smoothly. The bordering of figures and pictures is quite a difficult and laborious task. But the most artistic and skilled activities are the fixing of *jari* materials on the drawn figures through the main body *(jami)* of the cloth. Fixing of *jari* on the figures inside the main body of *sari or ghagra,* whatever it be, is an extremely subtle job, involving much of hardship, skills and accuracy. This is the work whereui the designers expressed their artistic motifs and perfections which they learned from their kins and fellow friends through years of apprenticeship. *Jari* embroidery continues to be an arduous work requiring a few simple tools, and implements, a very good eyesight, and steady hands, a keen sense of proportion and beauty. The technology of *jari* work can be mastered only with years of practice, and all the expert *jari* designers of today joined the profession at a very young age as apprentices. It is needless to say that, the reputation *of jari* embroidery as an artistic craft is the product of accumulated expertise gained through repetitive use of tested techniques generation after generation.

The artisans of *jari* work and their entire production system is guided essentially by verbal testimonies, thus fall under the category of little tradition i.e. *lokachar* or *desi* culture. Neither for this art nor for organization of production they do not have any written records. For productive techniques the artisans are entirely depend on the knowledge and the experience of their elders. In the matter of artistic skills the artisans fall back upon the memory of their elders. They are the expert of this artistic knowledge system. This artistic activity has been continuing as a system of oral tradition.

Place of Manufacturing :

The manufacturing of *jari* work is mainly done in small workshops maintained by the local entrepreneurs, known as *ustagars.* The workshop is known as *karkhuna,* where the artisans of all categories work together. The workshop is provided with light (electric or kerosene lamp) and musical apparatus like FM radio, cassette player and T.V. etc. for cheap entertainment of the workers from their monotonous nature of work.

Jari work is also done in individual households, where family members, both boys and girls as well as men and women, are engaged in this craft preparation. Their wage rate depends upon the nature of work as per contact made with the *ustagar* earlier.

Types of *Jari* Work :

Jari work is a popular term prevalent among the artisans as well as among the common people too. It includes varieties of hand embroidery. On the basis of nature, types and materials used in the work, hand embroidery is divided into various types, viz. *arir-kaj* (pictographic work or *mutia*), *Jarir-kaj* (stitching work or *jardarji*), *badgerkaj* (embroiding and engraving on badge), *rakhir-kaj* (embossing and embroidery on *rakhi)* etc. Among these works *jarirkaj* and *arir-kaj* are traditional as well as age old, exclusively used for decorating women's and men's garments and other cloth items. In recent times *jari* work is being done to decorate the bed cover, pillow cover and curtain. While the *rakhir kaj* and *badger-kaj* are exclusively the new ventures of the artisans to popularize their craft in competitive global market.

The most popular dress items with which the artisans work are *sari, ghagra-chunri, churidar, jacket, kurta, dopatta, brassiere* etc. Mainly the silk, nylon and other synthetic fabrics (garments) are used for hand embroidery.

OBSERVATION

The jari work is a hand embroidery. The *jari* embroiders of different parts of India employ almost the same techniques for production of their craft. The materials used for this craft are *kasap, tiki, resamdouri, sifandouri, builen, dobka, chir, moti, pipe, kutri, makhmal,* and *gulli.* The most common tools for this craft preparation are *khoka, dhadda, samsera, arir-such, kaichi* and *files.*

Generally, a rectangular wooden frame is prepared by setting length and breadthwise called *adda* and *samsera* respectively. This rectangular frame is then placed over the four wooden stands called *khoka.* After preparing the frame the border of the cloth is set with the frame by stretching its sides and then designs are drawn on the cloth for decoration with the embroidery skills.

The *jari* works are of various types, like *arir-kaj, jartr-kaj, badger-kaj, rakhir-kaj* etc. The most important dress items on which the artisans work for embroidery are *sari, ghagra-chunni, Churidur, jacket, kurta, kamij, d-patta,* etc. Usually the silk and nylon clothes are used *for jari* work. The manufacturing of *jari* work is done both in workshops as well as in individual households.

4

Structure and Organization of Production

In West Bengal the *jari* industry, i.e., the craft of embroidery is entirely controlled by the Marwari *mahajans* or traders of Calcutta These traders are retailers as well as wholesalers, who have shops mostly located at Barabazar or Newmarket of Calcutta. Below the Marwari *mahajans* there are petty *mahajans* or middlemen of the locality, who control the artisans. The petty *mahajans* are popularly known as *boro-ustagar*. Under the *boro-ustagar* there are some *chhoto-ustagar* at the village level. Below them there are artisans who perform the art of *jari* embroidery. There are three categories of artisans, vix. master artisan *(dorji)*. Skilled artisan *(karigar)* and semi-skilled apprentices *(mujur)*. The manufacturing of *jari* embroidery is done in small workshop called *karkhana* where the male *dorji*, *karigar* and *majur* are working together. But when the *jari* embroidery is done in individual households there the family members including girls and women who have the knowledge of the art of embroidery are engaged in production system. For *jari* work the *ustagar* prepare and select the model of a design with the help of a designer *(Nakshagar)* and instruct the master artisans and skilled artisans to do embroidery work on the cloth. The apprentices assist the master and skilled artisans to complete the work in time and thereby learned the artistic or practical knowledge of this craft production.

Under the existing system the traders *(mahajans)* supply bare cloths to middlemen *(ustagar)* living in the villages. *ustagars* have their own shades or workshops *(karkhana),* where they engage the artisans and workers. They are paid on hourly wage basis *(nakri).* Some big *ustagar* engage smaller middlemen *(chhoto-ustagar)* and also individual households for production. Thus the finished *jari* work passes through one or more levels of middlemen or *ustagar* until it reaches to the traders or *mahajans.* The marketing of *jari* designed garments and other cloth items is exclusively controlled by the *mahajans,* where the *ustagars* who are also the entrepreneurs of this craft production have no role to play. It has been reported that in West Bengal, the whole *jari* industry is regulated and controlled by the traders *(mahajans)* of Bara-Bazar in Calcutta.

According to prevalent system, bare cloths are supplied by the traders to *Boro Ustagars* and told them to decorate the cloths with the help of hand embroidery (*jari* work) as per demands of the market. The designing of embroidery is being done by the *ustagars* with the help of expert designers and finally instruct the.skilled artisans to complete the work. Then the finished products passes again through one or two levels of *ustagars* (middlemen) and finally reaches to the traders again for sell. It is pertinent to note here that, the traders *(mahajans)* gain much out of its sell in the market. The margin of the middlemen (*ustagars*) is also quite lucrative. While the earning of the artisans and workers *(karigar)* is much less.

Since *jari worked* garments are highly favoured by the women of northern, western and central parts of India, so there is a limited consumption of *jari* embroidered garments in Calcutta market. Thus the large portion of the products goes to Rajasthan (80%), Delhi (10%) and Bombay (10%). There is also a high demand of this craft in international market, particularly in gulf countries. The margin of the traders is about 30 per cent to 40 per cent and sometimes more than the above figures. While the margin of the middlemen varies between 10 per cent to 20 per cent depending upon the demands of the craft.

In Calcutta under the existing practice of *jari* embroidery the supply of cloths which are to be embroidered comes through the garment shops of the marwaris and some of which are big concerns. The owners of these shops are licensed dealers. The jari artisans who actually produce craft of embroidery are not employees of these business concerns, but work on piece rate basis. The artisans even do not know the whereabouts of the marwari traders for whom they producc the goods. The owners of garment shop places order with a middleman *(ustagar)* and supplies the required cloth items to get them embroidered. The *ustagar* is to get his remuneration i.e. the profit at an agreed rate. It is the task of the *Ustagar* who gets the order, to produce the craft of embroidery in his workshop with the help of artisans *(karigars)* working under him. Actually the *ustagar* is acting as a middleman who maintains a relation between traders at one side and artisans on the other. So far his roles are concerned around the craft *of jari* embroidery is in a sense an entrepreneur. The artisans or karigars working under a *ustagar* in the workshop are virtually his employees, but legally they are 'self employed' *jari* artisans (workers).

In case of household production the *ustagar* supply the cloths and raw materials to individual artisans who work in home with their family members. These category of artisans get their remuneration at agreed rates from the ustagars who initially got the order from the *mahajan.* Thus, there is, an extensive division of labour behind the production of *jari* craft. The customer or users who buys the craft from garment shop is the joint product of many hands. The *jari* artisans who are the real producers of this artistic craft, however, remains unknown to the customers. Their work of high quality actually enhances the reputation of *ustagars* and finally the *mahajans* from whom the customers purchased the *jari* designed garments and other items. The *jari* artisans rarely produce their crafts for direct sale to the customers. Actually they produce goods for *ustagars* who supply the products to *mahajans* for sell in the market. So to *mahajans* as well as to customers the *jari* artisans are unknown fellows and the hard artistic works of many hands behind the craft is thus invisible. The outline of the prevailaing system of *jari* embroidery works in Bengal (Calcutta and Moffusil areas) given above makes it clear that the thousands of *jari* designers or artisans working in *jari* workshops under *Ustagars* are self employed by name only. Actually they sell their labour to the owners of the workshop (ustagars) and also to the traders (mahajans) of this craft on a fixed or agreed rate of remuneration. In that respect, they are akin to the *jari* workers who work on a piece rate basis in their respective households.

The *jari* artisans differ from the industrial workers in respect to their mode of existence. The industrial workers do not own the tools of production, but the *jari* artisans, particularly the *ustagars* (previously an expert artisan) those are owners of their workshops do own all the tools of production. Even the *jari* workers who work in their respective households are also possessing all the tools required tor this craft production. Only the *karigars* who work in workshop donot possess the tools. Again the industrial workers work together in hundreds within the same factory compound and often under the same roof and they are controlled through the formal bureaucratic system and organized by the trade unions. While the *jari* artisans work in hundreds of separate small workshops and in .thousands of different families scattered over a wider area. Owing to all these differences the agitation programme of the *jari* workers for better wage and benefits does not develop. This is perhaps the main lacuna behind the formation of trade unionism of the *jari* workers.

The most important aspect of *jari* work which deserves special attention is the prevalence of extensive unemployment in this small scale home based industry. The *jari* artisans or workers do not get adequate employment throughout the year, because the demand of *jari* worked garments is highly seasonal one. During the particular period, specially at the time of socio-religious ceremonies of Indian people, the *jari* artisans have more work. But during the lean season, they may have to seat idle for want of any serious work. During the slack season, their income becomes negligible, and their misery during such period can be imaginable. However, in recent times, two factors which may, to some extent, compensate the fall of demand of the craft of *jari* work. One is the diversification of embroidery designs on varieties of dress items and production of *jari* designed *Rakhi* and *Badge* for obtaining the wider market. The other is the possibility of exporting *jari* designed garments and other items to foreign countries. The export possibility of *jari* craft till now is at best of the wills of the Mahajans. The export market of Indian *jari* craft can not be expected to extend so much in the near future until and unless the *jari* or embroidery industry is free from its excessive dependence on the *mahajans* and on the internal market. Today, pressed between the fanatic rise in price of *jari* designed garments and the control of *mahajans* on this craft production, the *jari* embroidery industry is steadily heading towards a grave crisis. In human terms, what is at stake is the employment, earning and livelihood of thousands of people. In cultural terms what is endangered is the crisis of expansion of an artistic channel through which the Indian mind expressed its sense of beauty for ages. Is it not high time for our planners and government to find out a means for ensuring this age-old artistic small industry's survival ?

FINDINGS

The *jari* embroidery industry in West Bengal is exclusively controlled by the Marwari *mahajans* of Calcutta. Below the *mahajans* there are *ustagars*. The ustagars are of two types i.e. the big or *boro ustagars* and small or *chhoto ustagars*. Under the *ustagars* there are many artisans. The artisans are of three categories, viz. master artisan or *darji,* skilled artisan or *karigar* and apprentice or *majur.* The *ustagars* control the artisans. Among the artisans there are both men and women as well as boys and girls.

According to the existing system the *mahajans* supply bare cloths to the *ustagars* for embroidery designing. The *ustagar* made profit from the *mahajan* at an agreed rate. The *ustagars* have their own workshops or *karkhana,* where they engage artisans to work on hourly wage basis. Some *ustagars* engage smaller middlemen or *chhoto ustagar* who distribute works to the individual artisan families and paid remuneration on the contact basis. Under such a system the *ustagars* not only supply the cloths but also the raw materials to the artisan families. The finished *jari* products once again passes from *karigar* to *ustagar* at the village level and finally to *mahajan* at the city level. The marketing of the *jari* craft is exclusively regulated by the *mahajans* or traders of the city. They are both wholesellers and retailers.

The *jari* embroidery work is highly seasonal. In recent times the two facts to some extent compensate the seaqsonality of this artistic craft. One is the diversification *of jari* designing not only on garments, but also on other items. While the other is the popularization of *jari* embroidery products at the international market. So far the marketing trend is concerned the export cannot be expected to extend so much, until and unless the *jari* industry is free from exclusive dependence on the internal market and the wills of the *mahajans*.

5

The Entrepreneurs and The Enterprise

The Entrepreneurs of *Jari* Embroidery

Earlier there was no question of entrepreneurship in *jari* embroidery as it was largely patronized by the rulers and aristocrats. Only since the revival of self-employment and private economic activities and their subsequent momentum have given the scope of emerging enterpreneurs to promote the growth of *jari* work. But the role of *jari* entrepreneurs in process of economic and social change has uptill now largely been neglected in academic discipline. To begin with I will clarify the concept of entrepreneurship in relation to *jari* industry which is the subject-matter of the present research. In economic terms, the ideal type entrepreneur is regarded as an active *homo economicus :* Who as an owner plans an enterprise, successfully founds it, independently and responsibly leads it, and whereby takes personal risks or capital risks. The entrepreneurial activity sets a dynamic economic process in motion. The most important attributes of an entrepreneur are creative as well as innovative behaviour and leadership qualities. Their function is to recognize and exploit new possibilities in the area of economy The entrepreneur acts more by ambitions than by intellectual aims The enterprises are to be regarded as complex interwoven system of events, whose collective activities strengthen the process of change. Thus the entrepreneurs are the social actors who are substantially involved informing and influencing this system (Schumpeter : 1936).

The entrepreneurs do not act in a vacuum, but are embedded in structures of social relations, and therefore are not autonomous, but act within a social environment. Social relationships are the necessary pre-requisite for successful business dealings. In order to fulfil economic functions, social commitments are required. The nearest conception of profit orientation as the key characteristic of entrepreneurship does not go far enough. Firstly, profit is not an end in itself, but is simultaneously a 'centre of interest' which develops its own norms and thereby takes on a controlling function. (Simmel, 1994). Secondly, psychic profits, that is non-monetary incentives such as social recognition, are very important to the entrepreneurs. In order to provide security and risk minimization for entrepreneur several factors are required. These are creation of individual contacts with influencials, politicians, banks, authorities and organization of interest groups in order to achieve advantageous situation in economic, legal and social spheres. The entrepreneur, therefore, has interests which reach far beyond the economic sphere, even if they do serve to secure his economic activities. As an interest act or entrepreneur, therefore, also promotes economic and social change (Heberer, 1998). For healthy development in agriculture, industry, business and any sphere of an economy, there must be men and women, who possess drive ambition, foresight and imagination to break through the traditional barriers and transform theory into practice. Individual performing these functions are the entrepreneurs and their enterprising ability and skill is known as entrepreneurship (Kumar : 1996).

Now the question arises whether the ideal type entrepreneur the attributes of which set above is applicable in the context of *jari* industry in India. The western concept of entrepreneur is usually regarded as an autonomous individual in terms of the philosophy of enlightenment. Thus it has a limited applicability in Indian context for obvious reason, particularly for complexity of social system and inter-dependent relations between different stages of business dealings. Thus, here we will refer to entrepreneurs as those who have founded and now run private enterprises or privately owned business which they now on the whole manage and develop independently. This already demonstrates a great deal of innovation, as they are largely people, who now find themselves economically and socially risky. Entrepreneurship allows a high degree of autonomy and freedom to take decisions and responsibility for oneself, and also implies a leadership function. Entrepreneurs are not a single, homogeneous group. There are entrepreneurs running large, medium sized and small businesses. There are entrepreneurs whose origins lie in the wealthy family background and have significant connections, and those without such facilities and contacts.

Primarily there arc three groups of people who are associated with the *jari* industry in Bengal, vix. *mahajans* (traders), *ustagars* (middlemen) and *karigars* (artisans). Though *jari* industry is basically controlled by Marwari *mahajans* of Kolkata, yet they can not be regarded as entrepreneurs as they lack creativity, innovative behaviour, and leadership qualities to motivate the artisans for better production. They simply associated with the trading of *jari* products and their main goal is to enjoy the profits. These mahajans are the professional businessmen having business of various items including the *jari* craft. For trading of *jari* craft they exclusively depend on the *ustagars,* who supply them the *jari* products. The artisans who produce the *jari* crafts are under the control of *ustagars.* They know the *ustagars* as their master, guide and philosopher. The artisans heard about *mahajans,* but never saw them. Thus mahajan is a invisible trade controller. While *ustagars* collect order from the *mahajans,* prepare the designs, supply raw *(jari)* materials and engage artisans to complete the work of embroidery. Most of the *ustagar* had previously been employed as *jari* artisans or as managers of *jari* workshop. The *ustagars* are the real actors who are substantially involved in functioning of the system of *jari* embroidery industry. They are ambitious as well as risk takers. Only for getting order and bare cloth they depend on *mahajans,* but for production of *jari* craft they invest capital, raw material and employ the artisans. In this context they enjoy a higher degree of autonomy, have freedom to take decision and take responsibility as well risk. Thus in real sense of the term they are the entrepreneur of the *jari* work and their enterprising ability and skill may be called as entrepreneurship. The *ustagars* living in villages as well as in towns and for their business interest they maintain a contact with the traders of the city to get the orders. As per demands they invest their capital (raw materials and wage) and engage the artisans to produce the goods. The artisans are fully dependent on the *ustagars* for performing their arts and also for employment and earning. The *ustagars* are located in between the traders of the city and the artisans of the villages. So far their place and involvement is concerned they are no doubt the middlemen, but at the same time the actors and functionaries who actually have taken the initiative to flourish the craft of *jari* embroidery. The atisans producing the craft as per direction of the *ustagars*. Neither they have capital nor the idea of market of their products, simply they are the followers and practitioners. For the sake of their artistic craft production they are exclusively dependent upon *ustagars*. To them *usatagar* is the owner as well as the master.

Jari Entrepreneurship and Social Change :

The *jari* entrepreneurship has a significant impact in village society, resulting into social change. The term social change does not refer to mere alterations within the respective economic or social subsystem, but means change to the social structure or a system. Social structure constitute 'regularities', such as role behaviour, values, social stratification and so on. Social change is a highly complex and comprehensive process which is difficult to cover in the present context. We have, therefore, concentrated on the following aspects.

Earlier, even before a decade ago the *jari* work was considered as not a good occupation, thus the persons associated with the *jari* work used to enjoy low social position in village society. But today due to the growth of unemployment many people have accepted the *jari* embroidery as a means of their livelihood. The *ustagars* today by virtue of their economic position and the control over artisans enjoying power and prestige in village society. These upward mobile private entrepreneurs of *ustagars* category can be seen as the new business elite among the village Muslims. Traditionally a set of values and attitudes have been developed in and around the *jari* work. But the emerging entrepreneurial activities of the *jari ustagars* have changed the previous values and attitudes. A sort of economization of the value system is taking place. The rapid and comprehensive economic change due to growth of *jari* industry in some villages has effects on society which brings about social change. The most striking change is the development of a new business elite from below. It consist mainly of *jari* entrepreneurs who have become rich in the course of time. Because of different market opportunities, a gap in incomes has been developed which has led to polarization of *jari* entrepreneurs. This affect the solidarity among them. This lack of solidarity among the *ustagars* (entrepreneurs) failed to constitute a corporate business body to complete with the *mahajans* or traders of the city.

The growth of *jari* entrepreneurship at the village level by the ustagars facilitates the process of change in economic system. This process automatically lead to change in social and political system of the village. In this context, the decisive question is whether *'middle class'* will develop out of this new economic elite and that might direct economic and social change at a wider context ? There is a hope that in long run a process of greater transformation will be generated through this self employed private economy and rise of the independent interest group.

The term "middle class" refers to a middle stratum, that is to groups such as private entrepreneurship, employees in higher or medium level positions, civil servants, professionals and the intelligentsia. Actually, the middle strum consists of heterogeneous group. In sociological literature the term *"middle class"* means the intellectual minority which provides leadership in every society. Nazmul Karim (1980), stated "For one to belong to middle class, one must have some kind of educational and cultural attainment. A tradesman or shopkeeper may belong to middle income group, or even the upper income group, yet he could not be taken as a member of the middle class, unless he has some kind of educational and cultural attainment". It has been observed that the *jari* entrepreneurs in general have a low educational standard and most of them previously been employed as *jari* artisans or as managers under some other senior *ustagars*. Their previous social background and low educational status does not allow to consider them as a component of middleclass in village society. Their socio-economic background also does not allow them to extend the progressive role in social transformation and moderrnization of the society. However, the present generation *jari* entrepreneurs *i.e.*, ambitious *ustagars* have a craze not only to develop their business but also to educate their children and family members for achieving high status and playing good roles in the society.

Entrepreneurial Behaviour — Individualism and Co-operation :

For a long time, it was generally believed that capitalism breed best in a ground of individualism. This was often based on the notion that industrialization in Europe was mainly achieved owing to the relationship between individualism and entrepreneurial behaviour (Dobb, 1978). Following this notion of the early European industrialists as independent, self made businessmen, many scholars have argued that cooperation in the line of caste, clan and kinship caused inhibitions on the development of "capitalist" activity in Asia (Goody, 1996). Following the economic rise of the East and South-east Asia in the past few decades, many studies started to challenge those earlier views on Asian entrepreneurs. In contrast to earlier views, they emphasized the aspect of cooperation as one of the key factors to explain Asia's business success. With regard to Asian entrepreneurs it is often argued that the joint family, kinship and caste have significant contribution to their economic success (Rutton, 1995).

A common feature of both the earlier and more recent approaches to entrepreneurship in Asia is that they discuss entrepreneurial behaviour in terms of individualism versus cooperation, assuming that some groups are culturally more inclined towards cooperation than others. My own study on *jari* entrepreneurs of Bengal indicate that these approaches are rather one-sided and that both cooperation and individualism are usually present among them, or even within one and the same entrepreneur. In order to substantiate this argument, I present below some of the findings of empirical studies on *jari* entrepreneurs living in four villages, belonging to Muslim community. The study was conducted among the *ustagars,* who are the owners of *jari* workshops located in their villages.

My research findings on *jari ustagars* and entrepreneurs of the villages of Howrah district in West Bengal shows the predominance of family unit as a form of economic cooperation. This unit of joint family and extended type of kinship institution has made it possible for its members to diversify their economic interest. Being a part of a family unit the system enabled them to mobilise financial, managerial and human resources needed for different types of activities in *jari* work. It is therefore, not uncommon to find that within one family, one member manages the business fund, another is a entrepreneur and some are directly involved in *jari* work *i.e.*, the production of the craft. The predominance of family organization among the entrepreneurs is not based on economic consideration only, but also based on an extended and inclusive notion of the concept of family. This notion of family involves a recognition of mutual kinship obligations and expectations which often include a large number of kins. For most of the entrepreneurs, the *Parivar* (Ghar), *Atmiya* (Khandan), *Kutumb* (Mehaman) - means an extended kinship unit which includes family members as well as other kins - consanguinal and affinal, the interests of whom are also taken care of in necessities. Co-operation within the family and kinship network is indeed an important aspect of business strategy of the *jari* entrepreneurs since the entire system of activities are very close, rather than open and flexible one. The transmission of knowledge relating to skills of craft production and business dealings are all operating under a very close system. A characteristic feature of the *jari* entrepreneurs is that they usually operate through their contacts within the known circle.

There is also an another dimension which I came to know through my conversation with the Muslim entrepreneurs of *jari* industry. Many of them stated that they operate their business independently and they donot make use of partnerships or other forms of co-operation in the field of activity either with kin members or with non-kin friends. Many of the entrepreneurs said repeatedly that they started their enterprises from scratch i.e. without any help from others, including parents and relatives. This self made achievement in business help us to draw a view that a section of *jari* entrepreneurs do not make use of any forms of economic organization than nuclear family farm. The research findings reveal that although a substantial number of the entrepreneurs live in a joint type of family structure, however, the most common type of family organization among the *jari* entrepreneurs is indeed the nuclear family. In most cases they separated from their parents soon after marriage in terms of hearth and property. This predominance of nuclear family form of business organization of *jari* entrepreneurs, does not mean that they did not receive support and assistance from their relatives and friends. This is most clearly shown by the fact that most of the present day young entrepreneurs were able to develop their business and *jari* workshop only because they received substantial help from their parents and kinsmen which often includes a piece of land for construction of a shed, some financial support, knowledge of artistic skills and technological knowhow for the production of *jari* craft. In addition to providing support and assistance during the initial set up phase of the business, in several cases family and kin members continued to play a major role for the first few years of a entrepreneur's life, particularly in sharing of orders and production process.

In several cases the sharing of orders often involving other enterprises owned by the relatives. In most instances these relationships are not between equal partners, but are of subcontracting nature, involving one larger and several smaller workshops of the entrepreneurs. In some cases a whole cluster of *ustagar's* workshops is interconnected with one another through sub-contracting ties. At the top of such a cluster stands one large enterprise of a *boro-ustagar,* who sub-contracts his orders among other small enterprises of *chhoto-ustagars,* provides them with working capital as well as raw materials for producing the goods i.e. the *jari* embroidery products. These sub-contracts are, therefore, often a convenient arrangement under which a big enterpreneur who contracts out a part of the production that relieves himself of the burden of labour management. This also helps him to devote time to receive more orders from the *mahajans.*

In most cases, co-operation in establishing and managing a *jari* enterprise is seen in the form of assistance, advice and subcontracting, while in other cases it is on the basis of partnerships. Although most of the entrepreneurs emphasize their reluctance to form partnerships owing to the question of profit sharing. Even then, there are some sort-term and ad hoc partnerships among the *jari* entrepreneurs. The partners involved on such cases were related to each other. This shows that the establishment of the form of business (economic) organization around *jari* embroidery beyond the family level is also a practice among the Muslim *jari* entrepreneurs in this part of Bengal.

The social background of the *jari* enterprise in Bengal shows that the idea of independent, self made businessmen is a myth in case of these Muslim *jari* entrepreneurs. This group of Muslim businessmen have in fact made use of wide variety of different forms of co-operation, simultaneously and successively, with regard to getting of order, capital, technology, labour and production of the crafts. By establishing sub-contracting system and short or long term partnerships with kin and non-kin members of village and locality the entrepreneurs are able to run their farms very successfully.

The approaches to analyse entrepreneurship in small and medium scale industries can be grouped into two categories. The scholars often analyse entrepreneurial behaviour in terms of individualism versus co-operation, assuming that some groups are culturally more inclined towards co-operation (Asian), while the others are self made (Western). In contrast to earlier views of West that emphasized the predominance of co-operation as a key factor to explain Asia's backwardness, more recent notions stress the pre-dominance of family and other forms of business organization as one of the key factors to explain Asia's economic development over past few decades.

My findings on *jari* entrepreneurs in Bengal (India) indicate, however, that both types of entrepreneurial behaviour are present among them. It is not much cooperation and individualism which explains successful or unsuccessful entrepreneurial behaviour, but the flexibility to adjust with the competitive system of economic organization is the most important.

FINDINGS

Earlier there was no question of entrepreneurship in *jari* embroidery industry. In recent times the growth of self-employment activities have given the scope of the emergence of entrepreneurs which promote the growth of *jari* work in southern parts of West Bengal. There are three groups of people who are directly associated with the *jari* embroidery industry, viz. *mahajans* or traders, *ustagars* or middle men; and *karigars* or artisans. The middlemen *ustagars* are the entrepreneurs of *jari* embroidery industry. The *ustagars* are the real actors who are substantially involved in functioning of the system of *jari* embroidery industry. The ustagars collect orders from the *mahajans* and prepare the designs, engage the artisans and provide them *jari* materials, to produce the craft and finally supply the products to the traders for sell. They are not only ambitious but also risk takers. The ustagars are the real entrepreneur of *jari* work and their enterprising ability and activity may be regarded as entrepreneurship. To traders the *ustagars* are the order receivers and order suppliers and to artisans they are their guide and philosopher.

The *jari* entrepreneurship has a significant impact in village society, as it has changed not only the village economy, but also the social behaviour. Even a decade before the people those who are associated with *jari* work were used to enjoy a low social position. But today they are getting recognition in village society and their economic and social roles are also taken into consideration. The *ustagars* today not only economically solvent but also influencing the village politics by virtue of their economic position and also of manpower, as a large number of artisans are under their control. But what is important to note here that these emerging *jari* entrepreneurs cannot be regarded as the member of middle class as they have low education.

The social background of *jari* entrepreneurs reveal that the family and kinship played a very important role as a form of economic co-operation. The institution of kinship obligation has made it possible for the members of the families to diversify their economic interest. Co-operation within the family and kinship network is indeed an important aspect of business strategy of the *jari* entrepreneurs since the entire system of production activities are very closely operated. The most characteristic feature of *jari* entrepreneurs is that they normally operate through their contacts within the known circle to maintain the business secrecy. There is also an another dimension which I observed among the *jari* entrepreneurs. Many of the *ustagars* operate their business independently and they do not make use of partnerships or other forms of economic co-operation in the field of activity. This self made achievement of *uatagars* help us to draw a view that a section of *jari* entrepreneurs do not make use of any form of economic organization than the help from family — nuclear or joint. In most cases support from the family has not been limited to providing economic help to the new enterprise but also to transfering knowledge and experience in regard to production process of *jari* craft and the management practices.

The *jari* entrepreneurs of a locality interacting with each other, particularly in sharing orders and production of goods. In most cases the sharing of orders are not between equal partners, but are of sub-contracting nature, involving interactions between a *boro-ustagars* with several *chhoto-ustagars*. It has been observed that both individualism and co-operation are very significant in the context of *jari* embroidery enterprise in Bengal.

6

The Economic Aspects of *Jari* Embroidery

Jari work as a small scale and cottage industry has a distinct place in India's economy. It gives employment to many people. Though exact statistical figure is not available about the number of *jari* embroiders in the country, yet it can be estimated that several lakhs of people depend on it for their subsistance. Besides, *jari* embroidery also generates income for several other categories of people in a indirect way. Among them there are carpenters who make the wooden frames needed for embroidery work, the tailors, the art designers and so on. Therefore, the prosperity of *jari* embroidery benefits a very large number of people who are directly or indirectly dependent on this craft production. The crisis of this industry, on the other hand, adversely affects not only the *jari* artisans and entrepreneurs, but many other people who have economic relation with this craft. An important aspect of the economics of *jari* embroidery that deserve attention is the unorganised nature of the craft makers and the prevalence of extensive disguised unemployment in this cottage industry. The *jari* artisans do not get adequate employment throughout the year. During the particular season or period, they may have more work than they can cope with, while during the other, they may have to sit idle for want of work. During the slack seasons, their earning becomes negligible and their misery during such seasons is easily imaginable.

In India the main markets of *jari* embroidery dress materials are Calcutta (Kolkata), Bombay (Mumbai), Jaipur and Delhi. The biggest market of work is Jaipur and Ajmer of Rajasthan, followed by Bombay (Mumbai) and Delhi. Calcutta (Kolkata) serve the needs of a small number of consumers of this state. The main users of *jari* products are the Marwaris and Sindhis. This is depending on the dress item and type of cloth on which *jari* work is done. Among the *jari* embroidery dress items maximum demand is for *gaghra-chunni,* next come the *saree*, followed by *churidar (salwar-kamij)* and others. The demand of *ghagra-chunni* is highest in Rajasthan and then in Bombay and Delhi. While the demand of *Saree* is highest in Bombay, Delhi and then in Rajasthan. The *churidar* or *salwar-kamij* is gaining popularily in everywhere. The demand of *jari* products in Calcutta is mainly confined for *Saree* and *churidar,* the sale of *gaghra-chunni* is very negligible in this city.

The style of *jari* work in Bombay (Mumbai), Delhi and Rajasthan varies considerably. In Bombay (Mumbai) demand is more for sophisticated designs and for the work on a good quality of synthetic cloths produced by the famous mills like Vimal, Garden etc. While in Delhi the demand is more for bright designs, with wide use of *tikki* and other glossy materials made of metal or plastic. The demand in Rajasthan is for heavy work on the glossy cloths such as tissue, ciphon etc. Demand for *jari* work on Banarasi and South Indian Silk sarees are also there, but due to high price of silk sarees the work on them are rather limited and done by the sophisticated and expert artisans.

The demand for *jari* worked garments is completely dependent on the marriage and festival seasons. This is true for all the places. For *gaghra-chunni* and *Saree* demand is maximum during those months when marriages take place among the Indian communities. Usually demand is high during winter and spring i.e. from October to April and much less during rainy season i.e. July to September. *Jari* worked garments have also the demand during Dewali, Holi, Onam and Eid festivals.

The major source of supply of the *jari* embroidery products to Bombay (Mumbai), Delhi and Rajasthan is Calcutta Barabazar. However, in all the places there are local artisans. What is important to note here that the *jari* embroiders i.e. the artisans who produce the craft either for Calcutta or for other markets are mostly the Muslim artisans of Bengal. The traders *(mahajans)* who are dealing with the sell of *jari* products of various places visiting Calcutta and contacting the suppliers *(ustagars)* with the help of local *mahajans* of the city. Their visits to Calcutta depending on the volume of business of *jari* products. Traders of Rajasthan usually visit Calcutta almost every month during the peak season. While the traders of Bombay and Delhi visit Calcutta market once or twice a year as they depend mainly on the local workers of their place. Sometimes they placed the order to Calcutta suppliers on the basis of samples received from them. The mode of payment to suppliers of Calcutta (Kolkata) is both in credit and cash, but the credit is most common practice. The margin for the middlemen suppliers is nearly 15 per cent to 20 per cent. While the margin of wholeselers in Calcutta (Kolkata) as estimated by the *ustagars* was found between 20 per cent to 25 per cent.

There are two major inputs associated with the *jari* work. These are cloths and *jari* materials. The cloths are of various qualities consisting of synthetic materials and the silks. Among the synthetic materials the most notable are ciphon, jorget, polyester, tissue etc. While the most important silk types are South Indian and Banarasi which are considered as most expensive and quality variety. The cloths are normally supplied to the *ustagars* and then to *karigars* by the Calcutta traders. The traders procure the cloths from various parts of India through the dealers in Calcutta city. After *jari* work is done on the cloth, the *mahajans* or traders make profit on the cost of cloth also.

The *jari* materials are mostly procured from Surat of Gujrat, where these are exclusively manufactured. It is one of the traditional centre of production of *jari* materials. The production of *jari* materials is also one of the small scale sector. The raw materials used in manufacturing of *jari* materials arc copper, silver and thread-cotton or silk or polyester. Varieties of chemicals and processing machines are used for colour coating on the *jari* materials. The manufacturing of *jari* materials also employs thousands of workers and their works are highly skilled. These skilled work force for manufacturing the *jari* materials are not available in Bengal, as a matter of fact the Bengal artisan embroiders depending on market to procure them for iheir artistic works. As per existing system the *ustagars* provide *jari* materials to the *karigars* for work. After the *jari* work is done on the cloth they supply the products to the traders. So the *ustagar* entrepreneurs make profit on the cost of *jari* materials also.

So far the profits and earnings are concerned among different groups involved in *jari* industry, it was noted that the incomes of traders and ustagars are quite lucrative. But the earning of artisans are much less. It is estimated that the margin of the traders is about 20 per cent to 25 per cent and for ustagars it is about 15 per cent to 20 per cent. Average monthly income of a ustagar is usually of Rs. 8000/-, but a big and renowned ustagar even earn more than Rs. 20,000/- per month. There is no fixed wage rate for an artisan. The rate varies between Rs. 2/- to Rs. 8/- per hour, depending upon the skills and the nature of work of the artisan. The monthly income of an artisan varies between Rs. 1000/- to Rs. 2000/-, with an average of Rs. 1500/- only.

FINDINGS

Jari work as a small scale cottage industry has a distinct place in country's economy. Its gives employment to many people. *Jari* embroidery industry generates income and employment to various categories of people both direct and indirect ways. Among them there are traders, *jari* material manufacturers, entrepreneurs, art designers, embroiders and many others. The craft of *jari* embroidery has a good market at national and international levels. Therefore, the prosperity of this craft benefits a very large number of people and thereby contribute to our national economy. The problems and crisis of *jari* industry, on the other hand, adversely affects not only the *jari* entrepreneurs and artisans, but many other people who have direct and indirect relations with the production of this craft.

In India the main markets of *jari* embroidery products are Rajasthan, Delhi and Bombay (Mumbai) but the main supply is from Calcutta (Kolkata). This is due to the fact that the majority *jari* embroiderers i.e. the artisans are mostly residing in the hinterlands of Calcutta. The Bengali Muslim *jari* artisans are considered to be the best embroiders in the country. Many of these artisans also moved to Delhi, Bombay and other cities for producing the craft to meet the local needs.

The main cloth items on which the artisans perform *jari* embroidery are *ghagra-chunni, saree* and *salwar-kamij*. The cloths are either of synthetic materials or of silk. There is a limited consumption of *jari* products in Calcutta. But Calcutta is considered to be the main source of supply to other markets, where the demand of *jari* products are very high. The demand for *jari* embroidered cloth items depend much on the marriage and the ceremonial occasions. Thus the demand of *jari* products is very high during October to April and much low from July to September.

Since Calcutta (Kolkata) is considered to be the most important centre of production, the traders of various places, who are dealing with the sale of *jari* products are visiting Calcutta markets for establishing contact with the local traders and suppliers. Their visits to Calcutta markets depending on the volume of business of *jari* products. Sometimes they also placed the orders to the suppliers on the basis of samples received from them with the help of their messengers. The mode of payment to suppliers is both in credit as well as in cash. But the credit is the most common practice.

There are two major inputs associated with the *jari* work, viz. cloths and *jari* materials. The traders procure cloths from various parts of India through the dealers. For embroidery work both synthetic cloths and the silk cloths are used. The cloths are normally supplied to the *ustagars* by the traders. After the *jari* work is done with the help of *karigars* the *ustagars* send back the finished products to the traders for sale in the market. Thus the traders or *mahajans* make profit both for cloth and also for its *jari* designing.

The *jari* materials are procured by the ustagars from the market which are exclusively manufactured at Surat. As per existing system the ustagars supplied the *jari* materials to the *karigars* or artisans for embroidery work. After *jari* designing is done on the cloths by the karigar the ustagars collect them and send back to the traders. Thus the ustagars who are the entrepreneurs of the *jari* embroidery industry make profit both on the cost of *jari* materials and also on the designing of the finished products.

So far the profits and earnings of different groups of people involved in *jari* embroidery industry are concerned, it was observed that the profit of the traders is very high, and of the *ustagars* it is lucrative. But the income of the *karigars* or artisans who are the makers of the crafts is very meagre.

7

Socio-economic Profile of the *jari* Embroiders of Four Villages—Field Studies

The *jari* embroiders, i.e., the *jari* artisans constituted a sizeable occupational group in the fringe areas of the district of Howrah in West Bengal. They are mainly concentrated in Damjur, Sankrail, Panchla, and Bauria police stations of the said district. The area that I have selected for field study includes four villages located in above noted police stations of the district of Howrah. There are innumerable *jari* embroidery workshops in the said places. The number of *jari* embroiders who work in these workshops or engaged in this profession at their individual households are also numerous. Field survey in villages has revealed that there are as many as one fifth of the total employed persons are engaged in this work. *jari* embroidery, in those areas, is exclusively a male occupation, but in recent times the girls and womenfolk of a embroider's family render assistance by extending their hands in the process embroidery craft production. Among the *jari* embroiders of those places about one-third are owners *(ustagars)* of *jari* workshop, whether big or small, and about two-thirds are salaried or wage-earner embroiders *(karigars* and *majurs).* The designs which the embroiders follow in designing the garments are not taken or borrowed from any catalogues or design books, but created and invented by some expert artisans out of their aesthetic experience. Some local embroiders sometimes take the liberty of modifying the created deṣign of the expert artisans, and if the modified design catches the market, it gains the popularity.

The *jari* embroiders of Damjur, Sankrail, Panchla and Bauria have the reputation of being expert artisans, particularly in the matter of *ari and jari* works. The craft of *jari* embroidery in those areas have a very long history. The very name *arigram* (village of *jari* work) is usually utter in the context of villages of above noted places, which according to some very old *jari* artisans, is derived from the prevalence of good embroidery works and the embroiders in them.

The present embroiders of those places are quite heterogeneous in many respects. Few of them are the descendants of the embroiders, who introduced this craft preparation in those areas at remote past. Most of the present embroiders are belonging to Muslim community of different occupational and social background. There are a few Hindus among the embroiders belonging to various castes. The number of educated embroiders is very small. However, majority of the embroiders are literate. There are illiterate embroiders as well. A few of the embroiders specially, the *ustagars* are quite well to do. But many of the artisans are not financially well off.

When I decided to study the economic, social and cultural aspects of the lives of these embroiders, I did not have any clear idea about the size, composition and nature of this heterogeneous occupational groups. I, therefore, started to gather preliminary knowledge about this craft and craftmakers. Through preliminary field enquiry I could draw up my plan of work and take a decision to study the *jari* embroiders of four villages, of four different police stations of the district of Howrah, where *jari* work gaining much popularity in recent times. The villages where I have conducted intensive field studies for examining the socio-economico-cultural life of the *jari* embroiders are named as Dakshin Korola, Uttar Dhulagori, Sahapur and Paschim Bauria situated in Damjur, Sankrail, Panchla and Bauria police stations respectively. I took the help of local field assistants, who were kind enough to give me an idea about the number of *jari* workshops in those places, the number of artisans working in them, the number of *ustagars* (entrepreneurs) involved in this craft business etc. Equipped with all these basic ideas I decided to conduct intensive field studies among the *jari* artisans. For detailed enquiry I planned to take a fairly representative sample of 10 per cent of the universe. I also framed necessary questionnaires consisting of a bunch of factual and attitudinal questions, and interviewed 147 artisans included in the sample. The sample broadly reflects the features of the total artisan population of those areas.

Field studies were conducted in the artisan villages with the help of research assistants. It took us about a year, to complete the interviews, and in this part of work we also received generous help from the local artisans. The local influencials introduced us with the *jari* artisans and requested them to help in writing a book on them by answering our questions and supplying us with information we wanted. Thanks to this generous help to the local leaders and influencials by whom we could establish a rapport with the embroider artisans for eliciting the required information from them. They came to accept us and shown interest in understanding their problems. For the sake of our knowledge they demonstrated the techniques used by them in *jari* craft preparation. They were free to told me about their personal backgrounds and professional experiences and thereby furnished enough material for writing a number of case histories. Apart from interviews and case studies, we had the opportunity to observe the embroider artisans from a close angle and to know a good deal of their aspirations and frustrations, hopes and fears, joys and sorrows.

Religious Composition:

The *jari* embroiders of the area is a bi-religious and multi caste community. The religious composition of our sample (village wise) is shown in Table 7.1.

Table 7.1. Religious Composition of *Jari* Artisans

	Name of ReligionDakshin	Number of Artisans									
		Uttar Karola		Sahapur Dhulagori		Paschim Bauria				Total	
		No.	%	No.	%	No.	%	No.	%	No.	%
A.	Islam (Muslim)	29	100.00	25	56.82	42	100.00	31	96.88	127	86.39
B.	Hinduism (Hindu)			19	43.18	—	—		1 3.12	20	13.61
	Total	29	100.00	44	100.00	42	100.00	32	10000	147	100.00

Majority of the *jari* artisans are Muslims, who constituting 86.89 per cent of the total embroiders under study. These Muslim artisans of the villages engaged in this profession since very past as fathers and grandfathers of many of them were also involved with this craft making. While the Hindus constitute a very small proportion i.e. 13.61 per cent of total embroiders. Most of the Hindu embroiders are the first generation artisan as they themselve taken up this profession for the sake of earning. These Hindu artisans learned the art of embroidery' from their Muslim artisan neighbours. The Hindu artisans are belonging to the castes like Jogi, Napit, and Podh and other scheduled castes. It is to be noted here that among the Muslim *jari* artisans there are both the owners of the workshop i.e. the entrepreneurs *(ustagar)* as well as the workers of various categories *(darji, karigar, majur* etc.). While the Hindu *jari* artisans are mostly the workers It must be mentioned here that, of the four villages under study Hindu artisans are noticed mainly in the village Dhulagori.

Age Categories

The *jari* embroiders of our sample are belonging to different age groups. The agewise distribution of *jari* artisans (villagewise) is shown in Table 7.2.

The *majurs* or *boys* constitute the youngest section among the persons engaged in *jari* workshops. This section of child labour constitute 14.97 per cent of total *jari* artisans of our sample. The work of these *boys* or *majurs* consists in assisting the skilled

Table 7.2. Agewise Distribution of *Jari* Artisans

Age Group	No. of Artisans									
	Dakshin Karola		Uttar Dhulaguri		Sahapur		Paschim Bauria		Total	
	No.	%	No.	%	No.	%	No.	%	No.	%
-10 yrs	-	-	-	-	2	4.76	-	-	2	1.36
11-15 yrs	1	3.45	9	2046	8	19.05	2	6.25	20	13.61
16-20 yrs	3	10.34	1 1	25.00	4	9.52	5	15.62	23	15.65
21-25 yrs	3	10.34	10	22.73	4	9.52	7	21.88	24	16.33
26-30 yrs	6	20.69	7	15.90	10	23.81	7	21.88	30	20.41
31-35 yrs	2	6.91	1	02.27	7	16.67	4	12.50	14	9.52
36-40 yrs	3	10.34	1	02.27	3	7.14	5	15.62	12	8.16
41-45 yrs	1	3.45	-	-	3	7.14	2	6.25	6	4.08
46-50 yrs	3	10.34	2	04.55	1	2.39	-	-	6	4.08
5l-55 yrs	1	3.45	-	-	-	-	-	-	1	0.68
56-60 yrs	-	-	1	2.27	-	-	-	-	1	0.68
61-65 yrs	-	-	-	-	-	-	-	-	-	-
65 yrs and above	6	20.39	2	4.55	-	-	-	-	8	5.44
Total	29	100.00	44	100.00	42	100.00	32	100.00	147	100.00

artisans or *karigars* by doing all sorts of sundry jobs from keeping the workshop clean and tidy to bring tea and snacks etc. Actually, these *boys* are the future artisans in preparation, thus considered as apprentices in this profession. Their guardians have sent them to work in the workshops with the hope that their sons will learn the techniques of craft preparation in course of time and one day become fullfledged *jari karigars.* A few of these boys already acquired the skills of embroidary and started to work as *karigars.* The girl child who are at this stage of apprentice are not attending the workshop but learn the art from their close kinsmen at their home The youngest apprentice I found is only 9 years old. The overwhelming majority of the *jari* artisans are belonging to the age groups between 16 to 40 years who constitute about 70 per cent of the total artisans The oldest working *jari* artisan in our sample is aged 80 years. There are of course, older people who are still associated with this craft, but due to old age, they are no longer actively engaged in the actual work of embroidery. They are basically acting as advisers to the designers. Old people above 60 years are a very small population i.e. 5.44 per cent of the total artisan population. One reason behind this, is, I guess, that the embroiders work involves a constant straining of eyes, as a result, the eyesight becomes affected sooner than in many other occupations thus incapacitates a artisan from continuing to work as an effective *jari* designer.

Male and Female Artisans

The *jari* embroiders of the villages under

Table 7.3. Distribution of Sex of *Jari* Artisans

Name of Religion	Number of Artisans									
	Dakshin Karola		Uttar Dhulagori		Sahapur		Paschim		Total	
	No.	%	No.	%	No.	%	No.	%	No.	%
A. (Muslim)										
(a) Male	25	86.21	18	72.00	33	78.57	30	96.77	106	83.46
(b) Female	4	13.79	7	28.00	9	21.43	1	3.23	21	16.54
B. (Hindu)										
(a) Male	-	-	19	100.00	-	-	1	100.00	20	100.00
(b) Female	-	-	-	-	-	-	-	-	-	-
Total	29	-	44	-	42	-	32	-	147	-

investigation are both male and female. The sex distribution of the *jari* artisans belonging to our sample (village wise) is shown in Table 7.3.

Majority of the *jari* artisans are the male, who constitute 85.71 per cent of the total embroiders (Muslim and Hindu) of our sample. While the females constitute only 16.54 per cent of the total embroiders. It is also to be noted here that the female artisans are noticed only in Muslim community. However, there are some Hindu female artisans in other neighbouring villages.

Economic Status

The *jari* embroiders of our sample does not constitute a homogeneous mass from the ángle of economic status. The levels of income among the jari workers are presented in Table 7.4.

There is a wide disparity in the incomes of different *jari* workers. The owners of workshops *(ustagars)* earn a lot, while the *karigars* and *majurs* do not earn much. There are some good *karigars* (designers) who are quite well paid but the ordinary *karigars* get a meagre remuneration. It is very difficult to know how much actually the individual *jari* artisans earn per month, partly because their income varies from month to month and partly because they do not like to disclose their actual income. This is particularly the case with the affluent *jari* artisans, specially the *ustagars* deliberately make an understatement of their income owing to fear of income tax. Actually most of the *ustagars* are affluent

Table 7.4. Income Levels Among *Jari* Artisans

Monthly Income	No. of Artisans									
	Dakshin Karola		Uttar Dhulaguri		Sahapur		Paschim Bauria		Total	
	No.	%	No.	%	No.	%	No.	%	No.	%
Below Rs. 500	2	6.90	1	2.27	7	16.67	4	12.50	14	9.52
Rs. 500-1000	7	24.14	9	20.46	21	50.00	19	59.37	56	38.10
Rs. 1000-1500	3	10.34	9	20.46	6	14.29	5	15.63	23	15.65
Rs. 1500-2000	12	41.38	15	34.09	8	19.04	4	12.50	39	26.53
Rs. 2000-2500	2	6.90	3	6.81	-	-	-	-	5	3.40
Rs. 2500-3000	-	-	4	9.10	-	-	-	-	4	2.72
Above Rs. 3000	3	10.34	3	6.81	-	-	-	-	6	4.08
Total	29	100.00	44	100.00	42	100.00	32	100.00	147	100.00

who own two-storied buildings, T.V. sets, motorbikes and few of them even possess the cars. However, none of the *jari* ustagars reported a monthly income of more than Rs. 3,000/-. My observation of the standard of living among the *jari* embroiders *(karigars)* of the villages suggest that the overwhelming majority of them are not financially well off. This fact is also borne out by the data collected from field villages on different income levels of the embroiders of our sample. The data reveals that a great majority of the *jari* embroiders (89.80%) have a monthly income upto Rs. 2,000/- while only a few (10.20%) have income upto Rs. 3,000/- and above. Apart from the income level, another test of economic status of this artisan group, would be whether they want their children (next generation) to stay on in this profession. If embroidery is really a lucrative profession, the majority of present embroiders would like their sons or daughters to become future embroiders like them. But the truth is that only 30 per cent of our sample wants their sons to become embroiders. This aversion to train the next generation as embroiders coming from frustrating economic experience of the present generation embroiders. However, they admit that this embroidery work giving a scope of employment when unemployment is a great problem in their society. Majority of the *jari* artisans, particularly those who belong to the age category upto 15 years are the partial earners. Either they live in joint families or many working brothers live together with the parents so they together earn quite a significant amount and contribute to maintain the family.

Table 7.5. Child Labour Among *Jari* Artisans

Child Labour	Number of Artisans									
	Dakshin Karola		Uttar Dhulagori		Sahapur		Paschim Bauria		Total	
	No.	%	No.	%	No.	%	No.	%	No.	%
Upto to the age of 15 years	1	3.45	9	20.46	10	23.81	2	6.25	22	14.97
Total *Jari* artisans of the villages	29	-	44	-	42	-	32	-	147	-

Table 7.6. Sex Distribution Among Child *Jari* Artisans

Name of the Villages	No. of Artisans					
	Boys		Girls		Total	
	No.	%	No.	%	No.	%
1. Dakshin Korola	1	6.25	-	-	1	4.55
2. Uttar Dhulagori	7	43.75	2	33.33	9	40.91
3. Sahapur	6	37.50	4	66.67	10	45.45
4. Paschim Bauria	2	12.50	-	-	2	9.09
Total	16	72.73	6	27.27	22	100.00

Child Labour

Jari embroidery is exclusively a labour intensive home based industry. A significant number of child labour is also associated with this artistic work. The distribution of child labour in different villages is presented in Tables 7.5 & 7.6.

Among the 147 total *jari* artisans of our sample there are only 22 (14.97%) individuals who are upto the age of 15 years. Thus they may be regarded as child labour. Among these 22 child labours, 16 (72.73%) are boys and only 6 (27.27%) are girls. The boy child labours are mostly engaged in *jari* workshops (as apprentices), while the girls are learners and doing *jari* designing along with the other family members in their respective households.

Family Size :

Table 7.7 presents data pertaining to family size of the *jari* artisans under study.

The families of the *jari* artisans in many cases joint, but nuclear families are also quite frequent. The total number of families of our sample are 147 and the total persons in these families are 1045. There are on an average 7 members per family. In the case of joint families of the *jari* artisans, there are cases, where the father as well as his son or sons both are *jari* workers. Similarly there are families, where two or more brothers engaged in *jari* work are living together in the same family. The nuclear families are predominating among the middle aged *jari* workers.

Table 7.7. Family Size of *Jari* Artisans

Family size No. of Members (x)	Name of Villages								Total	
	Dakshin Korola		Uttar Dhulagori		Sahapur		Paschim Bauria			
	No. of families (f)	Total No. of persons (fx)	No. of families (f)	Total No. of persons (fx)	No. of families (f)	Total No. of persons (fx)	No. of families (f)	Total No. of persons (fx)	f	fx
1 member	-	-	1	1	-	-	-	-	1	1
2 members	-	-	-	-	1	2	-	-	1	2
3 "	1	3	-	-	2	6	-	-	3	9
4 "	7	28	5	20	1	4	3	12	16	64
5 "	5	25	8	40	9	45	6	30	28	140
6 "	1	6	9	54	11	66	3	18	24	144
7 "	5	35	4	28	6	42	3	21	18	126
8 "	1	8	5	40	3	24	5	40	14	112
9 "	7	63	5	45	5	45	1	9	18	162
10 "	1	10	4	40	2	20	4	40	11	110
11 "	-	-	-	-	-	-	1	11	1	11
12 "	-	-	1	12	-	-	4	48	5	60

Family size No. of Members (x)	Name of Villages								Total	
	Dakshin Korola		Uttar Dhulagori		Sahapur		Paschim Bauria			
	No. of families (f)	Total No. of persons (fx)	No. of families (f)	Total No. of persons (fx)	No. of families (f)	Total No. of persons (fx)	No. of families (f)	Total No. of persons (fx)	f	fx
13 "	1	13	-	-	2	26	2	26	5	65
14 "	-	-	-	-	-	-	-	-	-	-
15 "	-	-	-	-	-	-	-	-	-	-
16 "	-	-	-	-	-	-	-	-	-	-
17 "	-	-	-	-	-	-	-	-	-	-
18 "	-	-	-	-	-	-	-	-	-	-
19 "	-	-	1	19	-	-	-	-	1	19
20 "	-	-	1	20	-	-	-	-	1	20
Total	29	191	44	319	42	280	32	255	147	1045
Mean family size fx n.		6.59		7.25		6.66		7.96		7.12

Table 7.8. Marital Status of *Jari* Artisans

Marital Status	Dakshin Korola		Uttar Dhulagori		Sahapur		Paschim Bauria		Total	
	No.	%	No.	%	No.	%	No.	%	No.	%
Unmarried	5	17.24	27	61.36	22	52.38	13	40.62	67	45.58
Married	21	72.41	16	36.37	20	47.62	19	59.38	76	51.70
Widower/Widow	2	6.90	-	-	-	-	-	-	2	1.36
Divorced/Separated	1	3.45	1	2.27	-	-	-	-	2	1.36
Total	29	100.00	44	100.00	42	100.00	32	100.00	147	100.00

Marital Status :

The marital status of the *jari* artisans of our sample furnished in Table 7.8.

The data presented in Table 7.8. reveals that 51.70 per cent of the artisans are married and 45.58 per cent are unmarried. The percentages of widower/ widow and divorced/separated are quite low among the *jari* artisans. Since quite a good number of boys and youths are engaged in this craft making the unmarried artisans represent a significant number in our sample. The mean age at marriage of male and female *jari* artisans are 23 years and 17 years respectively.

Educational Status

The educational level of *jari* embroiders under study is significantly very low. In many cases a *jari* artisan joins this profession at a very young age as an apprentice, and thus his/her schooling is terminated after he/she has read upto class III or IV. Therefore, it is no wonder, that there would be a few among them who are of *madhyamik* or *Uccha* madhyamik (higher secondary) or graduate degree holders. Among the *jari* artisans of our sample only 2 (1.36%) are graduates and only 1 (0.68%) is a post-graduate degree holder. There are only 11 (7.48%) artisans who have passed Madhyamik and Ucchamadhyamik examinations. The number of *jari* artisans in the sample who have the educational background of primary and secondary standards are 53 (36,06%) and 41 (27.89%) respectively. Quite a good number of *jari* artisans (26.13%) are really illiterates. There are a few among the *jari* artisans who have a working knowledge of English and Accountancy. Table 7.9 presents field data pertaining to educational status of the *jari* artisans.

The *jari* embroiders under study regard their lack of education as a hardship, thus today sending the children of their families to schools and colleges with an aspiration to make the next generation more educated than the present one. They feel that for raising their craft to a higher level of efficiency and sophistication and for profitability educational development among them is very necessary. It is also true that the educated members of the *jari* artisan families usually prefer to leave the craft for going in some other service. The spread of education have two divergent effects on embroidery craft. On one hand, it is likely to strengthen the craft because educated artisans will be able to handle the technical and business aspects of it more efficiently. While on the other hand, it is likely to weaken the craft by moving away the educated next generation from the family occupation and thus depriving from the expertise of the art of embroidery. This could accumulate only through successive generations pursuing this occupation.

School-going and Non-School-going Artisans

It has already been mentioned that there are 22 (14.97%) *jari* artisans who are below the age of 15 years, thus belonging to the stage of School-going age. The Table 7.10 presents data on school-going and non-school-going artisans belonging to our sample.

Table 7.9. Educational Status of *Jari* Artisans

Educational Status	No. of Artisans: Dakshin Kotola				Uttar Dhulagori						Sahapur								Paschim Bauria														Total	
	Muslim		Hindu		Muslim				Hindu		Muslim				Hinhdu				Muslim				Hindu											
	Male		Female		Male		Female		Male		Female		Male		Female		Male		Female		Male		Female		Male		Female		Male		Female			
	No	%	No	%	No	%	No	%	No	%	No	%	No	%	No	%	No	%	No	%	No	%	No	%	No	%	No	%	No	%	No	%	No	%
Illiterate	5	20.00	4	100.00	-	-	-	-	2	11.12	5	71 44	5	26.32	-	-	7	21.21	3	33.33	-	-	-	-	7	23.33	-	-	1	100.00	-	-	39	26.53
Primary upto Class IV	11	44.00	-	-	-	-	-	-	5	27.78	1	14.28	9	47 37	-	-	13	39 40	1	11.11	-	-	-	-	12	40.00	1	100 00	-	-	-	-	53	36.05
Secondary upto Class VIII	8	32.00	-	-	-	-	-	-	9	50.00	1	14.28	3	15 79	-	-	10	30.30	2	22.23	-	-	-	-	8	26.67	-	-	-	-	-	-	41	27.89
Higher Secondary (upto class XII)	1	4.00	-	-	-	-	-	-	1	5.55	-	-	1	5.26	-	-	2	6.06	3	33 00	-	-	-	-	3	10.00	-	-	-	-	-	-	11	7.48
Graduate (upto B.A., B.Sc., B. Com.)	-	-	-	-	-	-	-	-	1	5.55	-	-	-	-	-	-	1	3.03	-	-	-	-	-	-	-	-	-	-	-	-	-	-	2	1.36
Post Graduate (upto M.A., M.Sc., M. Com)	-	-	-	-	-	-	-	-	-	-	-	-	1	5.26	-	-	-	-	-	-	-	-	-	-	-	-	-	-	-	-	-	-	1	0.68
d	25	100.00	4	100.00	-	-	-	-	18	100.00	7	100 00	19	100.00	33	100.00	9	100.00	-	-	-	-	-	-	30	100.00	1	100.00	1	100.00	-	-	147	100.00

Table 7.10. School-going and Non-School-going Child *Jari* Artisans.

Name of villages	School-going Boys		Artisans Girls		Non-School-going Boys		Artisans Girls		Total	
	No.	%	No.	%	No.	%	No.	%	No.	%
1. Dakshin Kolrola	-	-	-	-	1	-	-	-	1	4.55
2. Uttar Dhulagori	1	-	-	-	6	-	2	-	9	40.91
3. Sahapur	4	–	2	-	2	-	2	-	10	45.45
4. Paschim Bauria	-	-	-	-	2	-	-	-	2	9.00
Total	5	22.73	2	9.09	11	50.00	4	18.18	22	100.00

Total school going child artisans 7 (31.82%)
Total non-school-going child artisans 15 (68.18%)

It is very sad to say that the young *jari* artisans are mostly the school droop-outs. Among the 22 child artisans only 7 (31.82%) are attending the school irregularly and the rest 15 (68.18%) are not pursuing their studies.

Forms of Entertainment

The embroider's work is a very monotonous one. The work starts at about 8 a.m. and continues till about 9 p.m. They enjoy one day's rest per week. The workshops in Dakshin Korola and Uttar Dhulagori area remain closed on Sunday, while in Sahapur and West Bauria the weekly rest day is on Monday. Actually the number of holidays in *jari* work are a few. This is not congenial to development of efficiency of the workers. In embroidery occupation, the present system of work leaves no scope of getting more holidays and the leisure hours.

Though the artisans often do not actually get sufficient time for rest and entertainment yet it does not mean that they are busy with their work all the times. For days, and even weeks together, they have some times to remain idle for want of any work. The leisure which the *jari* workers get everyday after the day's work is over, or on weekly holiday, or during the period of their prolonged involuntary idleness, is consumed mostly in attending to family and domestic business. The *jari* artisans usually spent their leisure time in gossiping and playing cards. Many of them (23.13%) are fond of films, particularly the Hindi films. A sizeable section among them (19.73%) watching T.V. programmes. Some of the *jari* artisans

Table 7.11. Forms of Entertainment of *Jari* Artisans

Forms of entertainments	Number of *Jari* Artisans who prefer it most									
	Dakshin Korola		Uttar Dhulagori		Sahapur		Paschim Bauria		Total	
	No.	%	No.	%	No.	%	No.	%	No.	%
Playing	5	17.24	18	40.92	8	19.05	6	18.75	37	25.17
Cinema	5	17.24	9	20.45	8	19.05	12	37.50	34	23.13
Watching TV	6	20.69	5	11.36	11	26.19	7	21.88	29	19.73
Reading of Books and Nespaper	-	-	-	-	3	7.14	-	-	3	2.04
Religious discussion	7	24.14	1	2.27	2	4.76	1	3.12	11	7.48
Music	-	-	7	15.91	1	2.38	-	-	8	5.44
No specific opinion	6	20.69	4	9.09	9	21.43	6	18.75	25	17.01
Total	29	100.00	44	100.00	42	100.00	32	100.00	147	100.00

(5.44%) like listening to music, specially the Hindi film music. Some others (7.48%) participate in religious discussion. Only a very few (2.04%) show interest in reading books, newspapers and magazines. What is interesting to note here that the majority of them (25.17%) participate in playing games (cricket and football) whenever they get sufficient leisure time during weekly rest day and other holidays. The forms of entertainment of the *jari* artisans under study is presented in Table 7.11.

FINDINGS

The *jari* embroiders constitute an occupational group. Its members are aware of being neglected. They have the feeling that this contributions are neglected by the government, ignored by the press and forgotten by the intellectuals, exploited by the *mahajans* with capital power and looked down upon by the educated gentry as downtrodden occupational group. The lot of *jari* embroiders in the study areas are no better than that of the *jari* artisans in other parts of the country. The economic problems, social practice and cultural attributes of 147 *jari* embroiders under study, of course, can not be regarded as identical with those of *jari* embroiders in other areas. But the study of the lives of these *jari* embroiders of four villages of the districts of Howrah, I hope, will throw some light on the social lives of the *jari* artisan community in general. The most significant aspects of their socio-economic life are as follows.

Majority of *jari* artisans of our sample are Muslims and only a very few are Hindus. The Muslim *jari* artisans are by tradition associated with this craft preparation since last few generations, while the Hindu *jari* embroiders are the first generation *karigars* learned the skills of this craft from their Muslim neighbours. Among the Muslim artisans there are both the owner of *jari* workshop or the entrepreneurs *(ustagars)* as well as the workers *(karigars).* But the Hindu *jari* artisans are mostly the *karigars.* The Hindu *jari* karigars usually belong to scheduled castes.

The most significant demographic features of the *jari* artisans are noted. The overwhelming majority of them are between the age of 16-40 years. However, there is a sizeable section among the *jari* artisans who are child labours. Among these child labours there are both boys as well as girls. Majority of the *jari* artisans are male. But there are some female artisans too.

From the angle of economic status it is seen that the *jari* artisans does not constitute a homogenous group. There is a wide disparity in incomes of different categories of artisans. The owners or *ustagars* earn a lot. But the *karigars* earn less. Among the *karigars* even there are differences of income depending upon their experience, nature and design of *jari* works. The child labours are mostly the apprentice, engaged in *jari* workshops to learn the art of embroidery thus getting a very minimum incentive. They are the partial earners.

The families of the *jari* artisans in most cases are of joint type. But nuclear type of families are also quite frequent. The average family size of the *jari* artisans is constituted by 7 members. The *jari* embroidery is an enterprise to many artisan families.

The *jari* artisans are mostly married. But the unmarried artisans are also found in good number. The mean age at marriage of the male and the female artisans are 23 years and 17 years respectively.

The educational level of *jari* artisans is significantly very low. Beside poverty the other significant reason is that a *jari* worker joins this profession at a very young age, thus his or her schooling is terminated at a very early age. The young *jari* artisans are mostly the school drop outs. Among the *jari* artisans 26.13 per cent are illiterate. The educational level of *jari* artisans reveal that, among them, 36.06 per cent having primary, 27.89 per cent secondary, 7.48 per cent higher secondary and 2.04 per cent graduate degree holders. The *jari* artisans regard their lack of education as a hardship to development. They feel that for raising their craft business and levels of living educational development among them is very necessary. Thus in recent times there has been a trend among the educated artisans to send their children to schools. Among the child *jari* labours only 31.82 per cent attending the school.

According to present system of work the *jari* artisans actually do not get sufficient time for rest and entertainment. The leisure which the *jari* embroiders get everyday after the day's work or on weekly holiday, is consumed in some popular entertainment activities, *viz.* watching Hindi films, listening Hindi film music and playing cricket or football, Chatting or gossiping is also very common among them to get a rid of their monotonous work.

8

Women *Jari* Embrodiers and Empowerment

Women have played a very significant but unaccountable role in developing the craft of *jari* embroidery and family economy. In patriarchal society where all social norms and cultural practices are geared to men's control in craft producing families women are forced to double up their vigour and enthusiasm to establish their identity through home managing and craft making. Entering into economic participation as *jari* artisan and be successful in it is a real challenge for women, whose exposure and mobility are limited. In this section an attempt is made to evaluate the performance of women *jari* embroiders hailing from field villages under investigation.

A woman who participates in *jari* embroidery and producing the craft with their artistic skills is called as a *lady karigar.* Similarly a woman who owns as well as operates the embroidery enterprise may be identified as women *jari* entrepreneur.

In all the four field villages it was noted that, in case of *jari* work at individual households (other than production at workshop) the women played a very significant role. Since it is the family enterprise the girls, maidens and even the married ladies of the artisan households learn the art of *jari* embroidery and participate in production process during their leisure time. Women *jari* embroiders are noted both among Muslims and also among some Hindu families who are involved in this craft preparation. But it is to be admitted here that there is not a single woman in the villages under enquiry who may be regarded as full-fledged woman *jari* entrepreneur. In field villages neither a *jari* enterprise nor its capital (even 50 per cent) is exclusively operated or owned by a woman. However, some *jari* ustagars (male entrepreneurs) involve a few women and placed them orders for production of the craft. The women who received the orders from ustagars are experienced *jari* artisans, they involve many other women of various households to complete the work and send back the finished products to the ustagars as per terms and conditions made earlier. These women who operated between ustagar at one hand and women karigars at the other may be considered as petty women entrepreneurs. These petty women entrepreneurs have been gradually emerging in field villages, particularly at Sahapur and Paschim Bauria. The age profile of the petty women entrepreneurs reveal that they are mostly in the age of 35 to 45 years. They are either widow or divorced/separated ladies taken upto this profession for the sake of their sustenance. These women are mostly trained for business by some voluntary bodies under self employment and women's empowerment scheme about which 1 shall discuss later.

While the age profile of women *jari* embroiders *(lady karigars)* reveal that a majority of them are either in the age group of 10-15 years or of 30-35 years. This is quite understandable, since during the said age groups either they are unmarried (10-15 years) or married (30-35 years) with sufficient home management experience. It is to be mentioned here that when the children are too young the women can not possibly think of devoting time to employment even it involves part-time work. In majority of the cases the women have entered in *jari* work operating in their families when their children are grown up and their mother in law and some others assist them in home management. They have entered into this time consuming artistic work only when they were convinced that they could do so. Since girls and women are not allowed to go to a workshop *(karkhana)* for *jari* work owing to the norms of *panlu* observance, a *ustagar* cannot think of employing a lady *karigar* for production. Thus the girls and women who are willing for self-employment in *jari* work exclusively depend on the family to fulfil their interest. The male members of the family approaching local *ustagars* for some works and after getting orders the works are assigned to the women. The women complete the works and handed over the finished products to the male members for sending back to *ustagars*. Under this system the women are only getting the wages as per contacts made between the ustagars and the male family members. In most of the cases the women are not handling their own income, as their wages are collected from the *ustagars* by the male members and utilized as family capital. Thus the contribution of the women artisans are not known to others. They are rather invisible hands both in craft making and home budget managing. Women's knowledge about the outside world is limited and their exposure is meagre due to lack of mobility, 'information' which is a vital input in self employment (*jari* embroidery) they obtained it from male members of the family. In this context the inferences which we derive from field studies are : (i) the married women are more prone to enter into *jari* work (self employment) than unmarried women, (ii) the middle aged married women who have the backing of their family members enter in a bigger way in the profession when compared to unmarried young women, (iii) it is the family economic condition (poverty) which forced the women, unmarried or married to take up *jari* work as a source of earning to support the family economy.

Marriage of girls being universal in Muslim and Hindu culture, they face uncertainty with regard to their future residence. Once a girl is married off she has to move her husband's place and this poses a dilemma whether they (*jari* working girls) should start the work again or leave that. This restrict the choice of partner only from that area where the married girls may cultivate their economic and artistic interests. Since in most of the areas of the district of Howrah the work of *jari* embroidery is prevalent, so the parents do not face a serious trouble to arrange their daughters' marriage within the vicinity. Only one consideration they usually maintain is to select a partner from a family whose members have also the knowledge and involvement in *jari* work. In the case of married women who have the backing of their family members in production of *jari* craft getting a smooth ground to cultivate their interest. The family enterprise of *jari* work give the women an opportunity of self-employment. Moreover, the wise women those who want to cash in their leisure, especially when the children are grown up, they devote sufficient time to engage themselves in the art of *jari* embroidery for the sake of learning.

The unmarried girls those are involved in *jari* work at their parental home unanimously opined that their economic participation and artistic skills not facing serious hindrance to their marriage. They said that it is not difficult to find suitable partners for them as the whole area of their habitation is a *jari* working zone in Bengal and many youths are involved in this profession. As a member of marginal class their expectations about bride groom is not high, so when the parents settle their partners having involvement in *jari* work they do not mind for that. Moreover, in such a marital arrangement they get an opportunity to cultivate their artistic activities and earn their livelihood in husband's or in law's home.

The education and training are two most important inputs in skill and entrepreneurial development. Education improve the quality of work of an artisan and also of an entrepreneurs as it enables them to acquire skills, helps in personnel management, financial management, market forecasting, so on and so forth. The study reveals that the maximum level of education among the women *jari* working group is Class VIII. There are many among the women *jari* workers who have only primary level of education. This educational backwardness creating a serious obstacle to their economic empowerment and self development even though they are half employed in *jari* work.

All the women *jari* artisans learnt the art of embroidery from their family members and they obtained their knowledge prior to entering the business. They felt that lack of technical knowledge for *jari* work is not at all a handicap to them for their self employment. They all learnt the artistic skills by observing and doing and through experience.

Coming to the role of decision making by the women *jari* embroiders it should be stressed that they do not feel the strain of decision making in respect to their work activities i.e. receiving of orders from *(ustagars,* performing the art of embroidery and production of goods as per orders, though they have never been socialized to perform these roles. Since in most of the cases the orders for work from ustagars are received by the male members of the family on behalf of women, the women usually getting a little scope to decide upon the matters. But all of them are found to be competent as men. While compiling the case studies the research has noted this very significant fact. So the question of a woman embroider's isolation and seclusion is not very much true.

The idea of the worker or entrepreneur being an inventor holds good for women *jari* artisans also. There are many women *jari* artisans who adopts innovative strategies in artistic styles, added new drawings and introduced new designs in the stitching and embroidery of garments etc. are the few examples to cite.

Family burden and self interest are the two most important driving forces behind a woman *jari* embroider. In the case of women *jari* artisans it is different type of self interest, namely fulfilment of ambitions like economic participation (independence), social status and maintenance of individuality. To most of the women *jari* artisans maintenance of individuality is their prime motive for entering into this artistic profession. Thus they all possess a forward looking mentality.

The petty women entrepreneurs who have started the *jari* embroidery business in contractual basis with the ustagars have also proved themselves as organization builders. They may be considered as good leaders and efficient organizers. These functions are performed very well by them, particularly those who have at least secondary level of education and getting support and cooperation from the family. The number of women *karigars* employed by them has also gone up consistently and which proves their capability of organizational behaviour. Organization building essentially calls for multifacted personality on the part of the organizer. In a male dominated society, where it is widely held that women could be easily cheated, and where many really do look forward to such an opportunity, women should be much more cautious than men in linking the various factors in business. But from field studies it is clear that women who have come in *jari* work business (though a few in number) are good organizers and efficient managers.

All the women *jari* artisans and petty entrepreneurs whom we studied clearly expressed that they do cooking and participating in maintenance of the family along with their works and business. On account of being 'earner' they have not been relieved of any of the household chores. When enquired about 'role conflict' all replied that they are able to combine both the roles successfully and efficiently. Firstly, because they are needy and ambitious thus do not mind to share the double burden and secondly, because they continue to play the traditional "house keeping' role of the women without questioning. Some of them of course expressed that they are finding it difficult to combine these two roles, but want to accommodate and adjust with the situation for the sake of family (*Ghar-Sansar*).

The women engaged in *jari* embroidery or business have been facing some problems in their works and activities. The most important problem faced by women is the absence of training institutes which would impart new technical, artistic and managerial skills rather than conventional age old informal technical training in the family. At present some Non-Government Organizations (NGO's) have come forward and started courses to train the women in *jari* work for starting business to strengthen the self employment scheme. But these are found to be inadequate, especially in equipping the women during crisis. No doubt the NAO's addresses the gender issues but give more stress on technical aspects of the business for the destituted women belonging to 'poorest of the poor' (below poverty level), than to develop the overall personality of women artisans and entrepreneurs of other social strata.

The other problem faced by women is the lack of information on job opportunity and market of the products. Since the entire mechanism of *jari* craft business is informal in nature, the women who have connections and rackets with the *(ustagars* through male members of the family are benefited, while the others are deprived. The Institution of parda prevalent in the villages is acting as a barrier to share the information whatever available in the locality. The NGO's working for women are not in a position to provide information to women embroiders owing to their lack of contact with the *ustagars,* those who regulates the entire *jari* activities at the village level. But the information network about the nature of demand and marketing system of *jari* products is very much needed for the sake of women *jari* artisans.

Another important problem faced by *jari* artisans, particularly the petty women entrepreneurs is the credit to start business. The nationalized reputed banks usually do not entertain the *jari* artisans and even the *jari* entrepreneurs. The Gramin Banks and

Cooperatives those who are willing to provide credit invariably suggests a woman to provide some form of gurantee, a proper business plan and her husband's or guardian's signature. Moreover, bank procedures are too lengthy and highly formal as well as combersome to understand for most women. As most of the women *jari* artisans or the petty entrepreneurs are either unmarried or divorced and separated women hailing from poor families with low educational background they are unable to get credits neither from bank nor from other institutions. Therefore, for the sake of credit they are totally dependent on non-institutional sources i.e. the local level moneylenders.

In the present context the women *jari* artisans inspite of showing interest have little practical knowledge since their contact with the outside world is limited. Since they are burdened with household responsibilities and regulated by the institution of parda, they are not in a position even to avail the opportunity of learning from various sources. Women from their childhood are oriented and prepared for being a good daughter, good sister, good housewife and good mother and not for employment and business career, so to make them bold, committed and risk loving is really difficult. The impediments to overcome on the socio-psychological side are much more severe than prevailing on the economic side. The women are trained for *jari* work at the family level, the outside training programmes whatever available for women are very few and far apart. These programmes give too much emphasis on imparting the required training of skills, thus hardly help them in developing positive attitude towards risk, innovation, marketing and sustainability. As a result the willing women do not pick up courage to venture out for self-employment. Inspite of hailing from such different surroundings the women artisans studied have proved their capabilities.

In the field villages, *jari* work is largely practiced not only by the youths and grown up boys, but the girls and women too take part in this artistic activities. The data reveal that in the sample on an average 16.54 per cent of girls and women are found as *jari* artisans. (28.00% in Uttar Dhulagori, 13.79% in Dakshin Korola, 21.43% in Sahapur and 3.23% in Paschim Bauria). It is noted that the girls or women who are engaged in this craft production are mostly of artisan *(karigar)* and apprentice categories. There are only a very few women, who are acting as petty entrepreneurs of this craft making business. These women artisans usually coming from poor families. When unemployment is at large in the country, the *jari* industry provides (if not more) employment opportunities as well as economic gain to a section of women. The women artisans usually work at their respective home. Due to the norms of seclusion *(parda)* which is prevalent in all Muslim villages, the girls and women are not allowed to work in the workshop *(karkhana)* which is the domain of the male artisans. Thus the girls and women cultivate their artistic activities inside their home. The male members of artisan families collect the orders from local *ustagars,* procure the tools and implements and involve girls and women of their households to assist them in completing the works. In some households the entire productive system is run by the girls and women. The girls who are engaged in *jari* work are mostly belonging to the age of 10-14 years, thus they may be regarded as child labour. These girls have accepted this profession owing to poor economic condition of the family and dropped out from school for the sake of earning. Similarly the women who are associated with the craft of *jari* embroidery are either divorce or separated or widow and destituted women, have taken up this profession for the sake of their sustenance.

Empowering Women through *Jari* Embroidery

Considering the economic, social and cultural significance of *jari* work, some non-government organization (NGO'S) have come forward to rescue the least organized *jari* artisans, specially the women embroiders to ensure better return for their labour In this context mention can be made about the works and activities of a voluntary body named Nari-O-Sishu-Kalyan-Kendra, situated in the village Khas Khamar of the district of Howrah in West Bengal. This organization has taken an initiative to implement a development project titled "Economic Empowerment of Women through *Jari* Embroidery Works" with the help of its own human and other infra-structural resources. The project work has been taken up through the financial assistance of South Asia Partnership India Trust (SAP), supported by

German Doctor for Developing countries. The main objectives of the said project are :

(i) To organize the women beneficiaries in small groups for creating awareness among them to promote small saving habit as well as to provide them credit for production and consumption.

(ii) To impart leadership training among seven (7) group leaders in organizational activities.

(iii) To train forty (40) women belonging to the traditional artisan families in *jari* embroidery for six (6) months in two (2) batches consisting of twenty (20) women in each batch.

(iv) To promote entrepreneural attitude among forty (40) beneficiaries for self-employment by giving them entrepreneural and management training for two (2) days in two (2) batches.

(v) To support the beneficiaries by supporting them necessary raw materials required for *jari* work and to train them in technological knowledge with the help of expert artisans of the locality.

The above project work has been operating since February, 1997, through which NSKK has performed the following activities :

(a) Group meetings of the beneficiaries were organized for creating their awareness.

(b) Leadership training were organized on cluster basis in two phases by the experts of NSKK.

(c) Fifteen (15) skilled and twentyfive (25) unskilled fresh beneficiaries were trained in fine embroidery (*jari* work. They were trained for six (6) months in two (2) batches. The first batch was of fifteen (15) and second batch was of twentyfive (25) heads.

(d) Beneficiaries were organized in two groups one in each village named Sahapur (a village under study) and Khaijapur. Training programmes were organized in the above two villages for the beneficiaries. They were trained in small saving which they have been started. It is planned that resources thus mobilized shall be re-cycled during the production period for matching with the SAP grant.

(e) Beneficiaries were trained to involve in self-employment. For which entrepreneural and management training were provided for two (2) days in two (2) batches. Required raw materials including the necessary tools and implements for work were also supplied to them for the sake of activities.

It was noted that in Sahapur village the women who received training in *jari* work and in entrepreneurship from 'I'NSKK are all involved in self-employment and they are doing well in their work and business activities.

FINDINGS

The *jari* embroidery provides employment opportunity as well as economic sustenance to many girls and women of the villages under study. The women *jari* artisans are mostly the widows or divorced or separated women, who have none to look after them. Some of them are living alone, while others have minor children or other dependants. They are socially distressed as they lack socio-economic security owing to poverty, widowhood, and lack of cordial relations with their close affinal and consanguinal kins. They feel insecure on account of their poverty, widowhood and lack of dependable interpersonal relations with the kinsmen. Due to all these reasons these poor women find their source of livelihood around less profitable *jari* work. Some girls too involve with the *jari* work on account of earning to support their family economy. The women artisans who are engaged in *jari* works mostly earn so little that it can hardly fulfil their basic needs. Further the educational level of the women *jari* workers are so low that lead them to live in isolation and seclusion, which is further strengthen owing to the socially imposed *parda* rules. All these facts functioning together as an intricate system to place them on the edge of socio-economic hierarchy.

The women who are engaged in *jari* work are less educated, secluded and isolated thus have no contact and communication with the external universe. As a result they are not aware of the importance of their craft and its trade value at national and international markets. They still depend on the traditional conventional tools and techniques to produce the crafts as they have no modern idea to improve the technology and marketing of their products for better return. Further, they exclusively depend on the male members of their family to receive the orders and to complete the works as desired by the male *ustagar* of the locality. Lack of solid organisation of the practitioners of the *jari* craft puts them in disadvantageous position in matters of procuring raw materials and marketing of their products at favourable price. The *jari* work has been practiced by the girls and women of marginal class as a last resort of their survival and is exploited by the business community to a maximum extent.

In the present context inspite of above constraints some women have come forward and started the business of *jari* embroidery as petty entrepreneurs and have proved their capabilities for self-employment. These women have adopted novel and innovative strategies to retain their business. The analysis of field data on women *jari* embroiders clearly reveal that the impediments they have been facing are much more on socio-psychological side rather than prevailing economic side for self-employment. The training programme available for women are few and in this context the project titled "Economic Empowerment of Women through *jari* Embroidery Works" run by a voluntary organisation named Nario-O-Sishu-Kalyan Kendra deserve special mention. It is observed that women if given the opportunity will prove to be good *jari* artisan and even the business owner of this craft production.

9

Embroidery Works and the Child Labour

Who is a Child ?

Under the UN convention, a child means every human being below the age of 18 years. Different laws have set varying age limits for the determination of what is a child. In conjunction with "labour", ILO Convention No. 138 places the general limit 15 years or under special national circumstances, 14 years (Fyfe, 1993).

According to Indian Constitution, child is a person who has not completed his or her 15 years of age (Legislation of India, 1979). According to Family Law and Child Marriage Restraint Act 1929, child means a person who if a male has not completed 21 years of age and if a female has not completed 18 years of age. According to Child Labour Prohibition and Regulation Act 1986, child means a person who has completed his 14 years of age.

What is Child Labour ?

The child work which is exploitative and threatens the health, welfare and development of children.

According to ILO regulation child labour is defined as, when children :

(i) Work too young : Many children start work at 6 or 7 years, for example in the *jari* work.

(ii) Work too long hours : In some cases 12-16 hours a day, like *jari* work.

(iii) Work for too little pay : as Rs.10- 15/- for a day, say in *jari* work.

(iv) Work in hazardous condition

(v) Work under slave-like arrangements.

In the context of child labour, a working definition of a child may be a person below the age limit of 15 years or in special circumstances 14 years, set by the Minimum Age Convention, 1973 (Fyfe, 1993).

Education and training is considered as the single most important remedy to the problem of child labour. Thus it is considered that the parents must be able to afford this, and of course schooling must be made available.

Child Labour in India :

Child labour has become a common phenomenon in India, and perhaps it is increasing with poverty and deteriorating living condition. Although India was one of the signatories of the convention on the Rights of the child, yet implementation of law is still very insignificant. The declaration and the convention remains mere as theory, far removed from the reality of their lives.

Various studies reveal that the problem of child labour has been growing in India. For example, 1981 Census puts the figure at 13.64 million, 1991 Census puts it at 14.5 million, 1993 National sample survey puts it at 17.3 million and the 1983 Operational Research Group of Boroda puts it at 44.0 million (Tripaathy, 1997).

The magnitude of the problem of child labour varies from rural to urban areas and from male to female child workers. The rate of child workers in rural areas is much more higher than the urban areas. However, in urban areas children work long hours, sometimes longer than their rural counterparts (Singh, 1942).

The number of child labour varies from organized sector to unorganized sector. In unorganized sector child labour exists in a greater extent due to the very nature of the sector. Child workers are also concentrated in some rural home based industries. In unorganized sector child workers are not organised on the line of trade unions and hence they cannot fight for their right. Children are thus found to be frequently working, as unorganized sector is not covered within the preview of the law of the land (Mittal, 1992).

The causes of child labour are varied and numerous. No single factor alone is responsible for such a problem. The various factors involved in child labour are all intrinsically interrelated. In a country like India, where over 40 per cent of the population is living in conditions of extreme poverty, in such a situation children work out of necessities and without their earnings the standard of living of their families would decline further (Ahuja, 1997).

The state/union territory wise distribution of child workers (in percentage) by sex in rural and urban areas are presented in the Table 9.1.

Table 9.1

State/Union Territory wise distribution (in percentage) of Child Workers by Sex, Rural and Urban Areas

S. No.	Region	Male		Female		Total
		Rural	Urban	Rural	Urban	
1.	India	59.83	6.60	31.31	2.26	100.00
2.	Andhra Pradesh	52.79	5.26	39.60	2.35	100.00
3.	Bihar	71.34	4.19	23.63	0.84	100.00
4.	Gujrat	61.20	8.34	28.81	1.65	100.00
5.	Himachal Pradesh	40.26	1.17	58.04	0.53	100.00
6.	Haryana	74.02	6.93	18.44	0.71	100.00
7.	Jammu & Kashmir	68.05	10.74	27.85	2.53	100.00
8.	Karnataka	54.97	8.36	33.11	3.66	100.00
9.	Kerala	42.77	8.60	40.80	7.83	100.00
10.	Madhya Pradesh	56.70	3.10	38.88	1.32	100.00
11.	Maharashtra	48.83	5.62	43.28	2.27	100.00
12.	Manipur	38.22	3.62	53.34	4.82	100.00
13.	Meghalaya	56.84	1.68	39.89	1.59	100.00
14.	Nagaland	41.68	2.51	54.20	1.61	100.00
15.	Orissa	71.49	3.76	23.37	1.38	100.00
16.	Punjab	83.36	12.18	3.63	0.78	100.00
17.	Rajasthan	62.13	5.52	21.13	1.22	100.00
18.	Sikkim	38.25	4.31	54.89	2.35	100.00

S. No.	Region	Male Rural	Male Urban	Female Rural	Female Urban	Total
19.	Tamil Nadu	45.98	10.71	37.32	5.99	100.00
20.	Tripura	69.09	2.17	25.70	3.04	100.00
21.	Uttar Pradesh	75.67	8.92	14.72	0.70	100.00
22.	West Bengal	73.50	8.33	14.51	3.66	100.00
23.	Andaman & Nicobor Islands	66.19	19.39	11.70	2.72	100.00
24.	Arunachal Pradesh	42.88	1.19	55.36	0.57	100.00
25.	Chandigarh	6.64	74.36	1.23	17.77	100.00
26.	Dadra & Nagar Haveli	50.93	2.38	44.27	2.42	100.00
27.	Delhi	5.87	80.12	2.63	11.38	100.00
28.	Goa Daman & Due	34.06	12.49	36.82	16.33	100.00
29.	Lakshdweep	25.81	25.81	35.48	12.90	100.00
30.	Mizoram	42.26	2.40	53.33	2.01	100.00

Source : Census of India, 1981, Series I, Part II/I-A. General Economic Tables B - 3 as abstracted from Triparthy (1997).

In India child labourers are concentrated in large number mostly in agriculture, construction works, carpet and shawl making handloom industry, embroidery works, gem cutting and polishing, lock making, fire works, glass and bangle making, tea stalls, restaurants and so on. They work for long hours. Many of them also work in hazardous condition. The child labourers in various industries working for a long time under a congested sheds facing a serious problem due to inadequate ventilation and insufficient lighting. Thus they usually suffered from several diseases like malnutrition, bronchitis, asthma, eye trouble and skin diseases. Anxiety, fear, depression and mental disturbance are quite common among them. In rural India it is the girl child who sees the smooth functioning of a house hold and also work in agricultural fields and home based industries. The working girls are mostly engaged in beedi making, gem polishing, coir making, embroidering, carpet making, garment finishing, bag making and fire works. In the case of self-employment girls are working usually as domestic servants. The working girls are not only getting meagre wages but also become the victims of sex violence. Girls in India engaged in a greater number in the world's oldest profession. According to UNICEF there are about 3,00,000 child prostitutes in India (Mukhopadhyay, 1995).

The Constitution of India has protected the interest of the child. It prohibits the employment of children in hazardous industry, secures the childhood and provides educational opportunity to all, at least constitutionally. Many acts were periodically enacted with a view to provide legal protection to children in various occupations. Among these laws Indian Factories Act (1981), Mines Act (1935), Employment of Children Act (1938), Plantation Labour Act (1851), Child Labour Regulation Act (1986) deserve special mention. National policy on child labour was formulated in 1987. A child labour cell was also established at National Labour Institute in 1990. In fact, all these governmental steps are to eliminate the problem of child labour from Indian soil. But unfortunately the impact of these laws on the society is not very appreciable. Thus, despite all these legal measures the problem of child-labour has become a grave.

Total eradication of child labour by legislation alone seems impossible and undesirable. In fact, the participation of people and of the society is very much needed to solve the problem. The poor parents should realize that they pay more than the income of their children in terms of their deprived childhood and snatching their opportunity to grow into a full adult according to their potentials. The employers on the other hand, should realize that employing child labour may reduce their primary wage cost, but in the long run it would cost them heavily in terms of efficiency and quality. Therefore, the raising of awareness and consciousness in the context of child labour is very important. Finally, Government should also come forward with a holistic approach to solve this problem.

Child Labour vis-a-vis Human Rights

Child labour is a rampant phenomenon in most of the underdeveloped or developing countries. Child exploitation has been prevalent in all society and culture throughout the history. There has been various attempts to prevent the exploitation of the child and the protection of their basic rights, but the fact is that, the exploitation of children is most common nowadays than even before. The general assembly of the United Nations hold the convention on the Rights of the Child on 20th Nobvember, 1989. The Universal Declaration of Human Rights (1948) and World Declaration and Plan of Action for the Survival, Protection and Development of children (1990) are the most important global management stratgies for the protection of child rights.

For dealing with the violation of human rights, several countries have established Human Rights Commission, like the Human Rights Commission in India. In many of the countries including India, have legislations like the child labour Prohibition and Regulation Act. Those legislations emphasize the regulation rather than prohibition of child labour. The legislations ban the employment of children in factories and restrict employment in so called hazardous works. But are otherwise permitted to enter in the labour force at any age and this is for considering the socio-economic situation of child labour force prevalent in the country. In a developing country like India child labour can legally be employed in small workshops, domestic service and likewise. Paradoxically, children can not work in large factories where working conditions are better and wages are higher. But they are permitted to work in cottage industries and in household sector where working conditions are not regulated, wages are low and working hours are long.

Child labour is on the increase in assembling works, cottage and export industries. Promoters of child labour argue that little and soft fingers of children and their clear eye sights are much more suitable than their adult counterparts. Child labours are considered as an asset in export oriented small industries as they can easily be laid off in case of slack demand without compensation, given the employer a competitive advantage.

Several opposition came from the western countries against the prevalence of child labour in developing countries. This is particularly reflected in carpet industry, garment industry and embroidery industry operating in south Asian countries. The governments of developing countries argue that the western countries are attempting to impose their own values and interests upon them, thus insisting on an end of child labour for business strategy. They argue that the child labour is not as onerous as it was in the west. They are not exploited, as they are the part of family labour, where they act as apprentices. Poor families need the income of their children for survival. Moreover, traditional small-scale industries need low wage labour to survive.

The social scientists are of opinion that better schooling and economic development would reduce the problem of child labour. They have the view that for elimination of child labour culture is not the barrier, but the economic condition of the family that depend on child labour for sustenance.

Child Labour in *Jari* Embroidery

The child labour in *jari* embroidery is very conspicous. A number of children both boys and girls are involved with this artistic craft production. Child labours are employed by the *ustagars* in their *jari* workshops and some are also engaged in household production Among the child labours in *jari* industry, there are apprentices as well as the artisans. A majority of the child labours got their job through relatives and friends and they are recruited on oral basis. Thus the recruitment process is highly informal as there is no written contact. It was found that the children gets the work in *jari* workshops by negotiation mostly on piece rate basis.

A brief overview on demographic and socio-economic aspects of child labour engaged in *jari* work at four villages under study are presented in Table 9.2.

Table 9.2

Demographic and Socio-Economic Profiles of Child Labour engaged in *Jari* Work (Total of four villages)

1.	Age Group	- upto 10 years	- 2 labours (9.09%)
		11-15 years	- 20 labours (90.91 %)
		Total - 22 child labours (14.97%)	
2.	Sex Category	- 16 (27.73%) boys 6 (27.27%) girls.	
3.	Family Background	-	Nuclear family, having the background of *jari* work, belonging to lower middle-class.
4.	Types of Job	-	Mainly engaged in manual works like cleaning and arranging cloths, thread cutting, stitching and fixing of *jari* materials etc.

5. Nature of Job	-	Apprentice i.e. the learner.	
6. Income per month	-	Rs. 200/- to Rs. 400/- (Child labours do not have clear idea about their income as they never handle the money by themselves. Their parents and relatives usually collect and handle the income.)	
7. Working Hours	-	Long hours. They do not have any fixed time of work, it can be as long as 8 to 12 hours a day.	
8. Marital Status	-	All are unmarried.	
9. Educational Status	-	(a)	Illiterate - 5 (22.73%)
		(b)	Primary upto Class IV - 9 (40.91%)
		(c)	Secondary upto Class VIII - 8 (36.36%)
10. Educational Accomplishment :			
		(a)	Continuing i.e. School-going - 7(31.82%)
		(b)	Discontinuing i.e. non-school going (Dropouts) - 15 (68.18%)

The empirical data reveals that there are a total of 22 (14.97%) child labour involved in *jari* work in four villages under study. Their age ranges between 10-15 years. These child *jari* workers came from artisan family background. They are trained and socialized in their respective families in such a way that they easily adjusted with the work activities at this early age. The parents of these child labours are of opinion that the economic condition and the social environment forced them to engage their children in this profession, as they need the income of the children. They also stated that considering the growing unemployment problem they have rightly taken the decision to involve the children in *jari* embroidery, so that they should not face unemployment at later stage. Most of the parents feel that by involving the children in *jari* work they have not committed any wrong, as they consider that the child workers are the part of family labour (in case of household production) where they act as learner of this artistic craft. The *ustagars* i.e. the promoters of *jari* embroidery work, those who engaged child labours in their workshop have argument that the soft fingers and clear vision of the children are very helpful for good *jari* designing. Since there is acute unemployment problem the *ustagars* taking the advantage of recruiting children in their workshop to run the business. They are also of the opinion tha the children those who engaged in their workshop are not exploited, but protected from futur unemployment. In their view it is not the questio of exploitation, but the protection of children fron starvation.

A study of educational status of child labour engaged in *jari* work at four field villages reveal tha 22.73 per cent of them are illiterate and 77.27 pe cent having education upto primary and secondar levels. Of the total child labourers recorded in fiel situation, 31.82 per cent of them are school-going an the rest 68.18 per cent arc non-school-going. Thes non-school-going child labours are mostly the schoo drop outs at their primary and secondary stage.

The educational status of child labours engage in *jari* embroidary industry at four villages unde study is noted in Tables 9.3 and 9.4.

Table. 9.3. Educational Status of Child Labours engaged in *jari* work.

Educational Status	Name of the Villages								Total
	Dakshin Karola		Uttar Dhulagori		Sahapur		Paschim Bauria		
	Male	Female	Male	Female	Male	Female	Male	Female	
Illiterate	-	-	1	-	1	2	1	-	5
Education Standard :									
(a) Class I									
(b) Class II	-	-	2	1	1	-	-	-	4
(c) Class III									
(d) Class IV	1	-	2	1	1	-	-	-	5
(e) Class V	-	-	-	-	-	2	1	-	3
(f) Class VI	-	-	2	-	1	-	-	-	3
(g) Class VII	-	-	-	-	1	-	-	-	1
(h) Class VIII	-	-	-	-	1	-	-	-	1
Total	1	-	7	2	6	4	2	-	22

Table. 9.4. Non-school-going and school-going child labours engaged in *jari* work

Non-school going and school going child labours	Name of the Villages								Total
	Dakshin Karola		Uttar Dhulagori		Sahapur		Paschim Bauria		
	Male	Female	Male	Female	Male	Female	Male	Female	
Non-school going child labours	1	-	6	2	2	2	2	-	15
School going child labours	-	-	1	-	4	2	-	-	7
Total	1		7	2	6	4	2	-	22

FINDINGS

Child labour has become a common phenomenon in India and perhaps it is increasing with unemployment, poverty and deteriorating living condition. Poverty and unemployment of adult members of the family push the children in difficult situation. Under such a situation children are forced to work in order to support their families for survival. It is estimated that there are about 20 million child labours in India. Child labours exist in a greater number in the unorganized sector. The involvement of child labours in home based small scale industries is very significant and in this context mention can be made about their engagement in *jari* embroidery. Child labour and human rights issue is highly debatable in contemporary times, particularly in developing countries. Thus there has been various attempts to prevent the exploitation of child labour and the protection of their basic rights. In India there are several legislations to protect the interest and rights of the child. Only legislations can not change the situation. Creating social awareness is the best step to make the situation better.

The empirical evidence on child labour engaged in *jari* work reflects the following facts. Majority of the child *jari* workers under study belong to the lower middle class. The parents of child labours usually do not consider that they are doing any wrong, rather a responsibility. They feel it is quite normal for a poor family. Parents do not hesitate to collect the wages of their children at the end of the week or the month from the employer *(ustagar)*. They never even think to inform their children about their earning, but give them a share from it as the pocket money. Parents have the view that, to be engaged the children in *jari* work, particularly in case of household production, the work load of the adult family members would be reduced and they could manage both economic and household activities together. The jan entrepreneurs or *ustagars* on the other hand have the view that their enterprise shows a positive result in generating sustainable employment and income to the children who have come to this profession. Thus they do not consider that the recruiting child labour in their workshop is an exploitation. Moreover, they consider it as a protection of the children. There is no doubt that there are some children (14.97%) who have engaged in *jari* work either in workshop or in household and doing this artistic activities skilfully without any question. They support their family by their meagre income. Majority of the child labours have an educational background of primary and secondary standards. Some (31.82%) of them still attending the school, while the others (68.18%) are dropped out. Many of them have still a desire to attend the school if they get that opportunity during their leisure time. Considering all these, should we consider the engagement of child labour in *jari* embroidery as exploitation ? Creating social awareness is the first step to make the situation better. This requires a holistic approach for formulation of policies to protect this traditional craft of *jari* embroidery and the child labours involved therein.

10

Portraits of *jari* Embroiders—Some Case Studies

A social and occupational group is composed of individuals and the lives of the individuals mirror the distinguishing features of that group. The *jari* embroidery as a craft and the embroiders as an occupational group of Damjur, Sankrail, Panchla and Bauria police stations of the district of Howrah in Bengal has its own distinguishing features. Its distinctiveness as an artisan group become clear to us if we have a close look at the lives of the individuals belonging to this artistic profession. The economic and family background as well as attitude and orientation of individual *jari* artisans are likely to tell us a tale for meaningful understanding of the *jari* embroiders than what emerges from statistical data about different aspects of their social life.

In this chapter I am presenting a bunch of case studies of individual *jari* artisans with an object to acquaint the readers with the natures and types of people who constitute the occupational group basing *jari* work. The individual cases were collected from field villages and also from neighbouring areas by adopting the 'case history' which is the most important technique of data collection in

Anthropological field study. The case studies have been presenting in a summarized form.

Case I

Asghar Ali of Dakshin Korola, aged about 20 yrs is a *jari karigar*. His father was a *jari* worker too. He and his younger brothers are continuing to work as karigars in a *jari* workshop of their village for couple of years. He was studying in Class VI when he joined in *jari* embroidery, and he had to give up his studies because of family economy. He had to maintain a family of seven persons including his aged parents, two brothers and two sisters. Asghar Ali has inherited along with his brothers, a single storeyed ancestral house and some landed property from their grand parents. He and his brothers together earn about Rs. 2500/- per month. Ashgar Ali and his brothers are in debt of Rs. 7,000/- which they had to take from a local mahajan for arranging their elder sister's marriage. Ashgar Ali is quite a popular figure as a good *jari* designer in the area. He has liberal views in social matters and is progressive in political outlook. He also visited Delhi and Bombay in connection with his profession.

Case 2

Israfil Middya of Dakshin Korola aged about 52 years but looks a little older. Originally a tailor and later joined as *jari* designer at the age of 25 years. He is married and has 4 sons and 3 daughters. He has an educational background only upto class III standard. His first two sons are also engaged in *jari* work, while other two sons and three daughters are in school. His intention is to train two sons as a good *jari* designer and let other two sons to join in industry as workers after their Madhyamik examination. He wants to see his daughters as a good housewife after their marriage and he has no intention to involve them in *jari* work. Israfil Midolya is one of the reputed *jari* designer in Korola and he is very scrupulously observe religious injunctions.

Case 3

Ali Alamgir is a young boy of 15 years. He is from the village Dakshin Korola. As the little income that accrues to his family from cultivation is highly inadequate to help all the family members (his parents, one widow aunt, one unmarried sister and one very young brother), he had to do something, to earn some money. A cousin of him is a *ustagar* and owns a workshop, and through him he secured the job of *karigar* in that workshop. His cousin helped him a lot to acquire the skills of *jari* embroidery. Now he is a good karigar, and earning about Rs. 1500/- per month, out of which he contributes to his father to maintain the family. He can read and write in Bengali. His ambition is to become the owner of a *jari* workshop in near future and for which he has also a plan to visit Delhi and Bombay to gather experience on the *jari* embroidery business. He would prefer to marry within his own community, but a village girl, because he does not have a high opinion of townfolk. He is very fond of film music, both Hindi as well as Bengali.

Case 4

Yunus Ali, aged 64 years of Dakshin Korola is a very respected person among the *jari* workers of this locality. Initially he was a popular *jari* designer, specialized in the area *jar-dargi* and *ari works*. But due to eye trouble and also for age, at present he is working as a manager in a *jari* workshop, which is owned by one of his close relative. Actually he is the guide as well as philosopher not only to the owner (ustagar) of the workshop, but also the artisans *(karigars)*. He lives in his own house along with his married sons. He is very honest and religious and has liberal views in socio-cultural matters. He is considered as one of a few senior *jari* artisan of Korola. He is very ambitious about the good future of *jari* industry in Bengal.

Case 5

Sayyad Ali, aged 48 years of Dakshin Korola is no longer a *jari* karigar today, though he once was in this profession. But his younger brother, who lives with him, is still a *jari* worker. Sayyad Ali left *jari* works at the age of 40 years after accumulating some money. After leaving *jari* work, he decided to start the *jari* embroidery business as a *ustagar*. Owing to his earlier relation with the *jari* entrepreneurs of the locality he was able to establish contacts with the *mahajans* of Kolkata. His maternal uncle himself a big *ustagar* who helped him a lot to develop his new business. From this modest beginning he has been able to become the owner of a small but profitable workshop. He read upto Class X and married to a girl of his locality who has education upto Class IX. Mr. Ali is very progressive in his outlook.

Case 6

Abul Basar a handsome youth of 24 years living in Uttar Dhulagori. He works as *karigar* in a pretty big workshop. He is educated upto secondary standard and is polished in manners. He comes from a respectable family and there are many well educated persons among his close relatives. He likes the *jari* work because of fashioning artistic things gives him pleasure. But he seems to be suffering from a complex, and feels that his relatives look down upon him because of his embroidery profession. He has a desire of being a big *ustagar* of his locality and thinks of opening a big workshop to provide employment to many *karigars* like him.

Case 7

Poresh Das of 28 years belongs to a Hindu caste of middle order and educated upto Class Vll originally of Uttar Dhulagori village under Sankrail police station of the district of Howrah. His father was a factory worker of Sankrail jute mill. After his father's death his family was in great difficulty. His family is composed of six members. One of his close Muslim friends, who is a *jari* artisan in Uttar Dhulagori, helped him to join as an apprentice in a embroider's workshop at the age of 16 years. Now he is a good *jari* designer. But he is suffering from a complex as his relatives look down upon him because of his involvement in *jari* work, which is considered as a profession of the Muslims. He is married and has two children.

Case 8

S.K. Sahajahan of 33 years of Uttar Dhulagori is very well known in the area lor his good skill in *ari* or *jar dargi* work. He is a married man living with his wife and two children. He is doing *ari* work for the last fifteen years. He can handle the very complex *ari* designing with beautiful artistic transparency. At first sight, one would mistake his *ari* work on a cloth as a paper picture or photograph, so artistic work made by him. As an individual he is very reserved in nature. The exact technique and skill which he uses for beautiful *ari* designing is closely guarded secret and he is reluctant to enlighten any one about the process followed by him, except in a very general way. As there is only a very few *ari* designers in the area in comparison with a large number of *jari* workers, his hands are always full with work, and that makes his income assured and steady.

Case 9

Gobinda Laskar of 18 years belong to a Hindu Scheduled caste living in Uttar Dhulagori. Owing to worse economic condition of his family, his father suggested him to take up *jari* work for the sake of earning. A ustagar of Uttar Dhulagori helped him to join in the *jari* workshop and trained him in *jari* embroidery. He is doing *jari* work for last four years. He is very much liked by his master ustagar for his sincerity and dedication. His parents and family members are also very happy as he earn about Rs. 400/- per week at this young age. His younger brother has also joined in *jari* work to support their meagre family income.

Case 10

13 years Raju Mondal of Uttar Dhulagori is an apprentice of *jari* work, working in a workshop under a *ustagar.* His brothers arc also the *jari karigars.* He joined in this profession at the age of 10 years owing to economic problems of his family. He has read only upto class II. He is living with his parents and two unmarried brothers. His father was also a *jari* designer. As a child he is very fond of games and sports. But his busy working schedule does not allow him to cultivate his sporting interest. His ambition is to be a good *jari* designer like his brothers.

Case 11

S.K. Sahabuddin is a boy of 13 years. He hails from the village Paschim Bauria. lie is the fourth son of his father who is a jobless mill mechanics. Sahabuddin is an apprentice working under a *ustagar* who also hails from the same village. Owing to lock out of Bauria Cotton Mill Sahabuddin's father was in trouble to run his family, thus he requested the owner of a *jari* workshop of his village to employ his son, as a 'boy' in his *karkhana.* The owner agreed as he needed a 'boy' to help the *karigars* in their work. Sahabuddin joined the workshop at the age of 11 years. His job mainly consists in keeping the embroidery-making implements neat and tidy and to clean the room of the workshop. He has, on occasions, also to collect finished products from various individual households as per direction of his master *ustagar.* His work is, however, not strenuous, and all that he has to do and to attend the owner to bring tea or *bidis* and cigarettes from the nearby stalls and to hand over those items to (*ustagars* and *karigars*, who needs them. His working hours extended from 8 a.m. to 8 p.m. with one hour break for lunch at 12 noon. He gets some leisure only after 8 p.m., when the workshop closes. Sahabuddin earns only Rs.200/- per month besides free food and lodging. He has no sparable time for play with other boys of his age group. His only recreation is seeing of film occasionally in the local cinema house and enjoying funny chats of the *karigars* in the brief intervals of their work. Life in the workshop is bit dull for him, but he knows that he has to prove himself as a good *jari karigar.* That prospect gives him impetus to endure the dullness that pervades his life today. Thus when there is no work to do, he watches the *karigars* fashioning of *jari* embroidery with skilled hands, as his aim is to become a *jari* artisan one day. Through his patience and perseverance Sahabuddin has now learned and acquired the art of embroidery and his *ustagar* is also ambitious about his future.

Case 12

Abir Ali of 30 years is a married man of Paschim Bauria. He is a *jari* artisan and associated with the *jari* work for last 16 years. His elder brother helped him to take up this profession as a means of their livelihood. He is earning about Rs. 450/-per week. His wife is also a *jari* designer working in her own home and earns about Rs.150/- per week. They have two kids. Abir Ali is of opinion that *jari* work gives them a source of earning and honest living.

Case 13

Kalam Ali aged about 40 years, but looks a little older living in Paschim Bauria. Once served as a factory worker as casual employee, then as an agricultural labourer. Later joined a *ustagar's* workshop, and in course of time became a *jari* karigar. He is married and has three sons and two daughters. He read only upto Class II. His sons and daughters are now in school. His intention is to train one of his sons as a *jari ustagar,* and let two others to develop as good *jari* designers.

Case 14

S.K. Azijul aged about 23 years, not yet married. He is from the village Paschim Bauria. His brother is a *jari ustagar* and he supervises the work of the *jari* designers of the workshop. Azijul knows the *jari* work and occasionally does work in his brother's workshop. He spends most of the time in organizational work of his brothers workshop. He is living with his married brother and widow mother. Azijul has read upto class IX. which helped him to look after the accounts of their *jari* workshop.

Case 15

34 years Farid Ali from Paschim Bauria is a reputed *jari* designer of the village. Poverty and unemployment forced him to search for self-employment. He found a berth in this craft making through a close relation who is also a *jari* artisan. He joined in this profession at the age of 14 years and became a good *jari* artisan owing to his artistic skills and vision. Due to prolong *jari* designing activities he

has been suffering from eye troubles and rheumatism. Thus he decided to leave the embroidery work and start the business of selling *jari* materials as which have good market in the locality. He actually developed a love for the craft and for the sake of which he has received recognition among his fellow artisans.

Case 16

Monirul Islam of 24 years is from Sahapur is now a petty *ustagar* of the village. Monirul started *jari* work at the age of 11 years and worked as a *karigar* for about 10 years. As a good karigar he was familiar with many *ustagars* of his locality. One of the *ustagar* suggested him to act as business partner on the basis of sub-contracting system. Monirul took this opportunity and open a small workshop near his own home. His younger brothers and cousins work as *karigar* in his workshop and getting support from the family to run the business. Monirul collects orders from the big *ustagars* and finished the works in his workshop with the help of family members and others. Owing to shortage of capital Monirul is not in a position to collect order directly from the *mahajans* of Calcutta, thus depending on local big ustagars for the purpose. Monirul has an ambition to act as an independent *ustagar* in near future. He has read upto class IX and living in family constituted by his widow mother, married elder brother, brother's wife, brother's son and two younger brothers.

Case 17

26 years old Sabir Ali of Sahapur is doing hand-

embroidery on various badge items and thus known as badger *karigar*. Earlier he was a *jari* artisan now shifted to badge designing which is a recent development in *jari* craft. Sabir worked under a badge *ustagar* named Musier Hussain on contact basis. Sabir has a small workshop for designing the badges with *jari* embroidery. In Sabir's workshop there are four *karigars* who belongs to the age group of 10-15 years. Sabir stated that his *karigars* (boys) are very efficient in designing of badges. He also worked with these karigars in his own workshop (*karkhana*). Sahir has education of Class VI standard. He is a bachelor living with his widow mother and a divorced sister. Sabir is very much ambitious to be an independent badge *ustagar* he has also a plan to visit Delhi in connection with his work and business.

Case 18

Maniul Hoque, a handsome youth of 17 years, works as *karigar* in a medium workshop of Sahapur. He read upto class VI and then joined in *jari* work as suggested by his father. At this young age Moniul acquired the skill of work and getting recognition as a good *jari* designer. He is living with his parents along with two younger brothers and a sister. Moniul has been planning to go to Bombay and to work there as *jari* artisan for more income. One of his cousin is also a *jari* designer of a big workshop in Bombay.

Case 19

Munsur Ali, a boy of 12 years, belongs to Sahapur. His father was an employee of Bauria Cotton Mill which is now closed for last couple of years. Owing to support the family Munsur joined in a workshop for learning the art of *jari* embroidery at the age of 9 years when he was a student of Class III. He started to learn the artistic skill along with his cousins and friends working in the workshop and within three years he became a *jari* karigar. He is now earning about Rs. 150/- per week. His other two elder brothers are also involve in *jari* work. His mother and younger sister too are engaged in *jari* embroidery at home. His father is managing the whole activities of this artistic profession. Munsur remarked that *jari* work provides them a source of employment otherwise they would face starvation.

Case 20

14 years old Khokan Ali of Sahapur is working as *jari* karigar in a workshop located at the village Khaskhamar which is very close to his home. His fater is also a *jari* embroider. Khokan Ali narrated that he joined in this profession at the age of 11 years as decided by his father. He learned the art of embroidery from his father as well as from *ustagar* and other senior *karigars* of the workshop with which he has been associated for last three years. At the time of joining in *jari* embroidery he was a student of Class IV. Khokan Ali stated that he had interest in education, but the family situation and social environment of the village did not allow him to continue his study. Since most of the boys of his age group were joined in *jari* work, so he was rather compelled to join in this profession for the fear of unemployment. Further, as most of his kin members

are also associated with the *jari* work so he had no other alternative option.

Case 21

In the context of women *jari* worker mention may be made about the life and works of Sabana Khatun living in Sahapur. She is a maiden of 22 years having been educated only upto Class IV standard. Due to some family troubles and poor economic condition of her natal family she has been engaged herself in *jari* work for last eight years. For the sake of her family she accepted this profession and initially worked as an apprentice under her own cousin who was one of the petty *ustagar* of the village. Sabana also received training from TNSKK for skill development in *jari* embroidery. Due to her devotion and experience in *jari* work, she is considered as one of the best women artisan of this craft production. As a result the other needy girls and women of her village seeking her advice. Sabana is in a position to inspire other girls and women of her locality to take up the art of *jari* embroidery for their self-employment. It is estimated that Sabana earns nearly Rs. 2000/- per month, which she spent for her family. Looking back she narrated various problems what she had to face initially for her self-employment in this craft making profession. As a young girl it was not possible for her to communicate with the other male artisans together necessary technological knowledge for this craft preparation Thus she had to depend on her close relations to acquire the skills and process of *jari* work. Even now she is facing trouble in communicating with the *ustagar* for the sake of her craft production, as she is unable to move freely in the village due to so called traditional *parda* rules. She remarked that, her training from NSKK helped her to change the outlook in relation to self-employment through *jari* work. Sabana is very glad to say that she is now economically independent.

Case 22

Begum Mariam of 28 years was born in a poor family of Sahapur. Her mother always kept her at home and taught to perform the domestic activities and the religious rites. When she was of sixteen years her parents arranged her marriage. But unfortunately her mother-in-law was very greedy and started demanding more money and other belongings from her parents as dowry. Her husband was also entirely on his mother's side. As a result after a year she came back to her parent's house with a male baby, because her position was no better than that of a maid servant in her husband's home. Her parents and brothers were very sympathetic and helped her to stand on her own feet for the sake of her son's future. Her elder brother was an expert *jari karigar*, who suggested her to learn the art of *jari* embroidery for self-reliance. She was very willingly participated in this craft work and within a few months she became a good lady *jari karigar*. At present she is running her craft making business very successfully and earning sufficiently. She has been fully engaged in *jari* work and spend her earning for the sake of family. Now Mariam safely said that she is quite independent at lease in economic sense. But being a woman she is still facing troubles to interact with the outside world as she has not been trained for such a purpose.

Case 23

14 years Manzura Khatun of Paschim Bauria is engaged in *jari* work along with her mother and sister in their own home. His father is also a *jari karigar*. Manzura narrated that when she was of 9 years old, her parents told her to learn the art of embroidery so that they can earn some money for the family. Accordingly she learnt the skill from her father and elder brother. At the time of joining in *jari* work Manzura was a student of Class III, thus she was not much interested to leave the school. Manzura stated that she not only perform the *jari* work at home but also assist her mother in various domestic activities, She is still very much interested to go to school, but her family situation does not allow her to cultivate such a noble interest. Manzura boldly stated that she was rather compelled to engage in *jari* work owing to economic condition and social outlook of her family.

Case 24

Bulbuli Khalun, aged 15 years, of Dakshin Korola narrated her daily life. She is living in a family consisting of parents, two brothers - one elder and another younger, and a sister. The parents brought her up in the traditional manner, following all the conventional rules prevalent in the village society. Her mother keeping her at home teaches to stitch and cook. While her father teaches her to pray *namaz*. She explained "my father is a busy person as he is working as *jari* artisan in a nearby workshop. I saw him for only a few hours in a day. My father took the same amount of interest in my affairs and in affairs of my brothers". Bulbuli narrated, "when I was a student of Class VI, for various reasons my parents told me to leave the school. Though I had no intention to leave my school, yet the situation forced me to do so at the age of 12 years and since then I am actively engaged in *jari* work as well as in domestic work of our home." She again narrated "my father is facing trouble to maintain our family owing to his meagre income, under such a situation myself and my elder brother doing *jari* work at our own home for the sake of earning." She remarked that being a boy my brother is in a position to devote much time for the craft work, while as a girl it is not possible for me to spent sufficient time on it as I have to perform the other domestic duties." Bulbuli concluded that "though I earn less than my brother, yet it is my pleasure to say that whatever I earn that I contribute to the family."

Case 25

Masuda Begum, a maiden of 23 years living in Uttar Dhulagori along with her widow mother and young siblings. She has education upto class Vll standard. Due to some family troubles and poor economic condition she has been engaged herself in *jari* work for last 10 years. She took up this profession through help and co-operation of some of her close neighbours. Her friends, obviously the girls, helped her to learn the skill of embroidery. Initially, she worked as an apprentice under a lady *jari* entrepreneur of her village and within a very short period she became a wellknown lady *jari karigar*. Due to patience, perseverance and devotion she is now considered as one of the good *jari* designer. It is estimated that Masuda earns about Rs. 2000/- per month. Her younger siblings are also the *jari* embroiders. Masuda has a plan to start a small *jari* workshop at her own home by engaging her sisters and other girls of the village and for which she is in search of help and cooperation from the *ustagars* of the locality.

FINDINGS

From the above case studies it is clear that the craft of *jari* embroidery provided employment to many needy persons, both male and female. The craft makers i.e. the embroiders are mostly hail from Muslim community. However, the Hindu artisans of different caste background are also not uncommon. Among the *jari* artisans there are both aged and middle-aged people as well as youths and children. Poverty and unemployment were the most common reasons for which most of the artisans had accepted this profession. The family environment and social situation were also played a major role to develop a congenial atmosphere for the growth of *jari* craft and self-fulfilment of the artisans.

The intervillage similarities as well as differences were also noted in connection with the work of *jari* embroidery and the artisan embroiders. The working hours of the *jari* artisans are almost same in all the villages, which consists of 8 a.m. to 8 p.m.; with a break of a hour for lunch at noon. In addition, they are allowed to go to take tea for half an hour once in morning and other in afternoon shift. But the nature and types of work as well as the involvement of labour force varies from village to village. In Uttar Dhulagori and Dakshin Korola both *ari* and *jari* works are prevalent and with which old aged, middle aged and young artisans are associated. Among the artisans there are Muslims as well as the Hindus. While in Paschim Bauria and Sahapur *jari* work is much more common than other types of hand embroidery. But what is to be noted here is that in addition to *jari* embroidery on dress materials, there are instances of embroidery work on *badges* and other types of articles like *rakhi, parda* etc. What is more important to be noted that in Paschim, Bauria and Sahapur *jari* artisans are mostly the youths and child labours.

The *jari* artisans of all the four villages have low educational status. But they learned and acquired the artistic skill of embroidery very minutely from their kins and friends who cultivate this craft work as a heritage of their tradition.

11

Jari Embroidery Works and *Jari* Embroiders : Problems, Prospects and Priorities

The aim of present study was to examine the social frame work of hand embroidery popularly known as *jari* work prevalent in West Bengal. The specific objectives were to find out the technology of craft for preparation, the structure and organizational aspects of production, the employer-employee relation, the economic and cultural significance of the craft, the socio-cultural life of the artisans and the problems of child labour. These issues are empirically tested and analysed in the foregoing sections on the basis of data collected from four villages of four different police stations of the district of Howrah in West Bengal. This section recapituates the main findings of the study and examines their sociological and anthropological implications in the context of problems and prospects of a traditional Indian craft.

I

The artistic craft of *jari* work is a hand embroidery, which is said to be originated first at Iran and propagated and developed at various parts of India under the patronage of medieval Muslim rulers. Earlier this artistic craft was primarily produced by the Muslim artisans and used by the Muslim and non-Muslim aristocrat class of Indian society. However, in contemporary times, both the Muslim and the non-Muslim artisans are involved in this craft making and the craft has attracted the attention of common masses of India and abroad. In India, *jari* work today is highly prevalent in Jaipur, Delhi, Bombay, Calcutta and their associated hinterlands. The district of Howrah in West Bengal is considered to be the largest centre of best *jari* designers of the country.

The *jari* embroiders of different parts of India employ almost the same techniques for production of their craft. The materials used for this craft making are : *kasap tiki, resamdouri, sifandouri, builen, dobka, chir, moti, pipe, kutri, makmal, gulli* etc. The most common tools for preparation of this craft are wooden frame or *dhadda, arior-such, kaichi, and files.* The *jari* works are of various types like *arir-kaj, jarir-kaj, badger-kaj, rakhir-kaj* etc. The most important clothing items on which the artisans doing embroidery designing are *sari, ghagra-chunni, churidar,* jacket, *kurta, kamij, do-patta* etc. Usually the silk and nylon cloths are used for *jari* embroidery. The manufacturing of *jari* craft is done both in workshops and also in individual households.

In West Bengal *jari* industry is exclusively controlled by the *Marwari mahajans* of Barobazar in Calcutta (Kolkata). Below them there are petty local level *mahajans* known as *ustagars*. The *ustagars* controlled the artisans. The artisans are of three categories, viz. master artisan or *darji,* skilled artisans or *karigar* and semi-skilled apprentices or *majurs.* Among the aritisans there are both men as well as women. Under the existing system the traders or *mahajans* supply bare clothes to middle men or *ustagars. ustagars* have their own workshops called *karkhana,* where they engage workers or *karigars* who are paid on hourly wage basis. Some ustagars engaged smaller middlemen or *chhoto-ustagar* who distribute works to individual artisans to work at their own households. Thus the finished *jari* crafts or goods passes through one or more levels of middle men, until it reaches to the traders or *mahajans.* Calcutta traders are both wholesellers and retailers. The marketing of this craft is exclusively controlled by the traders or *mahajans* of the city. The *jari* work is highly seasonal, thus the artisans do not get adequate employment throughout the year. In recent times the two factors to some extent compensate the fall of demand of the *jari* craft. One is the diversification of embroidery designing in various dress items and production of *jari* embroidery goods other than dress items, like *rakhi, badge, parda* etc. While the other is the ongoing demand of *jari* crafts among the people of other countries like middle-east, South Asia, South East Asia and parts of Europe. However, the export possibility of *jari* crafts till now is at best on the wills of *mahajans.* So far the marketing trend is concern the export market of Indian *jari* craft can not be expected to extend so much in near future until and unless the *jari* industry is free from its exclusive dependence on the *mahajans* and on the internal market.

Earlier there was no entrepreneurship in *jari* embroidery industry. But in recent times the growth of self-employment activities have given the scope for emergence of entrepreneurship in this artistic craft marking industry. There are three categories of people who are directly associated with the *jari* embroidery industry, viz. *mahajans, ustagars* and *karigars.* The *ustagars* are the entrepreneurs of this craft producing activities. They are not only the middle men, but the real actors who are substantially involved in functioning of the system *of jari* embroidery industry. The *ustagars* collect orders from the *mahajans* prepare the designs, supply embroidery materials, engage artisans to produce the craft and finally supply the finished goods to the traders for sell. They are not only ambitious, but the risk takers. The *ustagars* are the order receivers, order suppliers and also the guide of the artisans. They are the real entrepreneur of *jari* industry and their enterprising ability and activity thus be regarded as entrepreneurship. The empirical study reveals that the entrepreneurship of *jari* work has a significant impact in village society. The economic and social roles, of *jari* industry in the villages under study are very significant. The *ustagars* today not only economically solvent but also politically powerful by virtue of their economic position and control of manpower, since a large number of artisans are depending on them. The *ustagars* are not depending on them. The *ustagars* are no doubt entrepreneurs but they are not the members of middle class, as they have a very low educational status. The *ustagars* are either youths or middle aged men who have education only upto secondary or higher secondary levels. The most important characteristic feature of *jari* entrepreneurs is that they normally operate within the known circle to maintain the business secrecy. They usually operate their business independently and do not make use of partnership or other forms of economic co-operation in the field of activity. Occasionally, the *jari* entrepreneurs interact with each other for sharing orders and production of goods. In most cases the sharing of orders are not between equal partners but of subcontacting nature involving interactions between big *ustagars* with several small *ustagars* of the locality.

The craft of *jari* embroidery provided employment to many people. The *jari* embroiders constitute an occupational group. An intensive study was conducted among 147 *jari* embroiders of four different villages of the district of Howrah. The socio-economic life of the *jari* artisans depict some interesting features. Majority of *jari* embroiders under study are Muslims and only a few are Hindus belonging to lower caste order. Among the Muslim *jari* embroiders there are aged, youth and child artisans. The Muslim *jari* workers are by tradition associated with this craft work, while the Hindu *jari* workers are first generation embroiders. Among the *jari* artisans there are both *ustagars* as well as *karigars,* while the Hindu embroiders are mostly the *karigars.* The overwhelming majority of *jari* artisans are between the age group of 16-40 years. Among them there are more males and a few females. A section of *jari* workers are the child labourers. The child labourers are the apprentices of this artistic craft. Poverty and unemployment were the two most common reasons for which most of the *jari* workers accepted this profession. The *jari* artisans does not constitute a homogeneous economic group. There are wide disparity in incomes of different categories of artisans. The *ustagars* earn a lot, but the *karigars* earn less than the former. Among the *karigars* even there are differences in income depending upon their experience as well as nature and design of work. The *jari* embroidery is an enterprise to many artisan families. The average family size, among the *jari* artisans is of 7 members. Among them both joint and nuclear families are prevalent. The artisans are mostly married, but unmarried artisans are also quite frequent. The mean age at marriage of the male and female artisans are 23 years and 17 years respectively. The educational level of the *jari* artisans is significantly very low. Among them 26.53 per cent is illiterate. The educational level of the *jari* artisans shows that, 36.06 per cent having primary, 27.89 per cent secondary, 7.48 per cent higher secondary and only 2.04 per cent graduate levels of education. The young *jari* artisans are usually the school drop outs. Almost all the *jari* artisans regard their lack of education as a hardship to development. Only in recent times there has been a trend among the artisans, specially among the educated section, to send their children to schools and colleges. Among the child labourers only 31.82 per cent attending the school. The *jari* artisans actually do not get sufficient time for rest and entertainment. Whatever the leisure time available to them is usually consumed through some popular entertainment activities viz. watching Hindi cinema, listening Hindi film music, gossiping, chatting and playing.

The *jari* work provides employment opportunity not only to boys and men but girls and women too. Among the *jari* artisans under study there are some girls and women (16.54%). The women *jari* artisans are mostly widows, divorced or separated ladies. Majority of them are socially distressed, thus find their source of livelihood around less profitable *jari* embroidery. Some girls too involve with the *jari* work on account of earning to support their family economy. The girl and women *jari* artisans are all belonging to Muslim community. They are mostly the *karigars* work in their respective households under the direction of family members. The production in the household is cheap but at the same time more time consuming. In the individual households, the work is done mainly by the female members who are also required to do other household jobs. A female worker works for about eight to ten hours a day, that too with lot of intervals in between. Therefore, their working hours are irregular and the time to complete any job is very high. The female workers are both married and unmarried. The educational level of the girls and women artisans are very low which lead them to live in isolation, this is further strengthening due to the imposition *of parda* rules. Owing to their isolation and seclusion they are not aware about the importance of the craft and the significant roles they played for its preparation and production. They exclusively depend on male member of the family for receiving the orders and to complete the works as suggested by the male *ustagars* of their locality. The lack of solid organization of the practitioners of *jari* craft puts them in disadvantageous position in matters of procuring raw materials and marketing of their products at a favourable price. The *jari* work has been adopted by the girls and women of marginal class as a last resort of their survival and is exploited by the business community to a maximum extent. The analysis of field data on women *jari* embroiders clearly reveal that the impediments they have been facing are much more on socio-psychological side, rather than prevailing economic side for self-employment. Very recently a few experienced women *jari* artisans have come forward and started the business of *jari* embroidery as petty entrepreneurs and thereby proved their capabilities for self-employment. They have adopted novel and innovative strategies to retain their artistic skills and business. The training programme available for women *jari* workers are very few. The project titled "Economic Empowerment of Women Through *Jari* Embroidery Works" started by the Nari-O-Sishu-Kalyan-Kendra (a NGO) in Sahapur village deserve special mention as the benefits of which have been utilized by the many women artisans of the locality. It is observed that if the women given an opportunity they will prove themselves to be good *jari* artisans and even the business owner of this artistic craft production.

Jari work is a labour intensive small and home industry to which participation of child labour is very much pronounced. The empirical evidence on child labour engaged in *jari* embroidery reflects some interesting facts. The child workers under survey belong to lower-middle class, the parents of them do not consider that they are doing wrong to engage them in work at the early age. The parents have the feeling that it is quite normal for a poor family to utilize the child labour for the sake of earning. They have the view that to be engaged the children *in jari* work, specially in case of household production, the workload of the adult family members would be reduced and thereby they could manage both economic and household activites together. The parents opine that considering the problem of future unemployment, engaging children in *jari* work at the early age is rather their social responsibility. The *jari* ustagars those who engage child labours in their workshop have the view that their enterprise shows a positive result in generating sustainable employment and income to the children and also to youths who have come to this profession. They do not consider the recruiting child labour in workshops is an exploitation, but projected as protection. The field data reveals that 14.97 per cent of children are involved in the *jari* work. They are engaged either in *jari* workshop or in household production and doing the artistic works very skillfully. They support their family with their meagre income. These child labourers of *jari* work have an educational background upto primary and secondary standards.

Among these child labourers 68.18 per cent are school dropouts and 31.82 per cent attending schools, but very irregularly. Many of these child *jari* workers expressed their desire to attend schools and to continue education if they get an opportunity to cultivate such interest. Some of them even ready to attend the classes during their leisure time. Considering all these empirical facts should we consider the involvement of child labour in *jari* embroidery is an exploitation ? This awkward question has to be judged in the context of emerging human rights issue.

Case studies were conducted among the *jari* artisans of four different villages for obtaining indepth data on the production of *jari* craft and the life of the artisans. Some intra-village similarities as well as differences are noted. The working hours of the embroiders in the workshop are almost same in all the villages, which consists of 8 a.m. to 8 p.m. with a break of a hour at noon for lunch. In addition to lunch break they are allowed to go out for taking tea and snaks for half an hour both in morning and in afternoon shifts. But the nature and types of embroidery work as well as the labour force associated with them varies from village to village. In Dhulagari and Korola villages both *ari and jari* works are prevalent and the artisans associated with these works are both the aged as well as the youths. While in Paschim Bauria and Sahapur villages *jari* work is more common than other types of hand embroidery. In these villages *jari* embroidery is not only done on dress materials, but also on other items like *rakhi, badge* and *parda* etc. In these villages the *jari* artisans are primarily the youths and the child. Although the *jari* embroiders of all the four villages have low educational status, yet they learned and acquired the artistic skills of embroidery very minutely through their kins and friends who cultivate this craft work as a part of their heritage. The family environment and social situation of the *jari* workers played a major role in developing a congenial atmosphere for the growth of *jari* embroidery as an occupation which further helps in continuation of cultural heritage of the country.

The social position of *ari* and *jari* embroiders is somewhat low in village society under investigation. Due to backwardness in education and isolation the artisans have failed to acquire modern knowledge to develop their craft producing activities and thereby lagging to improve their social position further. Owing to lack of their contact with the external world they are not acquainted with the thoughts and ideas of progressive societies and modern market facilities. All these lead to the growth of conservative and undemonstrative attitude towards work and life lacking enthusiasm and quest of novelty. The artisans are looked down upon by the educated middle class families in their respective village and localities. The poor educated recklessly spending artisans are not able to improve their social position. Their work, levels of living and nature of recreation affects their psychology, personality, and style of life. The art of *jari* embroiders' has an adverse effect on health of the artisans. Rheumatism, loss of eye sight, indigestion are the most common health problems of the artisans. It is usually difficult for an experienced artisan to perform his work freely above the age of 40 years. Owing to close association with the *jari* work artisans are gradually cut off from other sources of employment opportunities. The *jari* work is also seasonal in nature. Embroidery worked (designed) garments are mainly used in socio-religious occasions viz. marriage and other socio-religious festivals. All these creating problems to sustain the life of an artisan. Moreover, *jari* work is a labour intensive industry. It is exclusively an unorganized sector of production where involvement of child labour is conspicuous, and which has lot of negative social consequences.

II

The craft of *jari* embroidery has a great economic, social and cultural significance. When unemployment is an ongoing problem in a developing country like India, the entrepreneurship of *jari* work by some experienced artisans *(ustagars)* provides employment opportunities as well as economic gain to a section of underprivileged people. Not only the poor artisans earn by making the craft but the traders also make lucrative profit out of this artistic product. The craft has both domestic and international markets. In India the biggest market of *jari* worked dress materials and other products are Jaipur, Delhi, Surat, Bombay and Calcutta. There has been a growing demand for *jari* embroidery products in various foreign countries, specially the gulf countries. The traditional craft of Indian hand embroidery popularly called *jari* work has economic, social and cultural relevance. It stands for the continuity of an old craft and artistic heritage of India.

The artisans of *jari* work and their entire production system is guided essentially by verbal testimonies, thus fall under the category of little tradition in India. Neither for their arts, nor for organization of production they do have written records. For techniques of production the artisans are entirely depending on knowledge, experience and memory of their elders. They are the experts of this indigenous artistic knowledge system. This artistic performance has been continuing as a system of oral tradition of India. It is the human resource of the country that sustain its growth and continuity.

III

Considering the economic and socio-cultural significance of the craft of *jari* embroidery, following recommendations can be suggested on the basis of this empirical study.

(1) It is necessary to preserve and encourage this small scaled entrepreneurship of *jari* embroidery industry.

(2) Proper documentation of the artistic craft of *jari* work and the life of the artisans of the country is an urgent need.

(3) The problems of the *jari* craft as well as the craft makers have to be solved through proper planning and management.

(A) Plan for Improvement of Manufacturing Process :

(1) Formation of some kind of co-operative is very essential for long term feasibility of this craft production,

(ii) To form a co-operative it is necessary to organize the *karigars* and the *ustagars* of a locality. The grassroot level village institutions like Panchayat and voluntary bodies (NGOs) may play the key roles to organize the artisans.

(iii) To form a co-operative it is necessary to constitute small groups among the artisans. 15 to 20 artisans of a village may together constitute a "artisan group". This group should start the manufacturing process in a organized manner under a supervisor (*ustagar*).

(iv) The supervisor must have the capability of introducing new designs and he should also be responsible for making liaison with the dealers and traders for receiving orders and deliver of finished goods.

(v) Preservation, codification and if possible computerization of *jari* designs are very necessary for inventing new designs and also for eliminating confusion about designs at the time of receiving orders.

(vi) Arrangement should be made to provide bank loans to the needy *jari* entrepreneurs and artisans for sustaining their enterprising abilities and artistic activities.

(vii) A networking system between artisans *(karigars),* entrepreneurs (*ustagars)* and traders *(mahajans)* must be developed and strengthened, as under present system all these three categories of people are working in isolation from one another.

(viii) The two most important factors should be taken into consideration for the future of *jari* craft. These are, price of the items produced and quality of the products.

(ix) It is also necessary to decide the mode of payment to the artisans (either on wage basis or on price rate basis) for developing commitments to their work.

(x) The income level of the artisans may be improved if number of stages involved in distribution network of the production is reduced.

(xi) The channel of distribution can be bypassed if the artisans of individual households contact directly with the main *(ustagars* or the dealers.

(xii) It is also necessary to constitute a dealer network at the village level to get an entry into the market.

(xiii) The problem of seasonality of *jari* work have to be tackled through diversification of *jari* designs. Along with the conventional system of *jari* work on saree, *ghagra-chunni* and veil, *jari* designing should also be done on various other items.

(xiv) Diversification of hand embroidery may be achieved by using cotton and silk threads instead of conventional *jari* thread.

(xv) For strengthening the production of the craft both workshops and individual artisan households have to be integrated. These sectors should come under a common project of production for the development of *jari* embroidery industry.

(xvi) In each workshop at least 20-25 *jari* workers should work together under a supervisor who must be an experience designer *(ustagar)*. And each workshop should have at least 5 frames.

(xvii) The individual artisan household, who has its own frame should work regularly, for more production.

(xviii) Since in the case of household production work is done mainly by the female artisans, who are also required to do other works. Thus, this sector needs to be organized properly.

(xix) A small women artisan group consisting of 10-15 members can be formed by involving female members of related families to work together. This is very necessary for better production within a limited time to compete in the market. A proper system has also to be worked out to record the hours put in by each worker for the sake of payment.

(xx) Training programmes for male and female artisans are also very necessary for improving the quality of skills of the artisans.

(B) Plan for Improvement of Marketing Process :

(i) More domestic and export market should be explored for greater prospect of *jari* craft and for which diversification of *jari* designing is very essential. There is a good demand for traditional Indian designing work at international market.

(ii) The marketing of the products shall be benefited if the local *ustagars* integrate with each other and establish their contacts directly with the retailers and wholesalers of Kolkata and other cities.

(iii) To achieve the objectives of improving income and working condition of the artisans, it is necessary to organise them as an occupational group. Their production should be sold in the market through the new system, which eliminates the number of middlemen involved in each stage.

(iv) It is important to devise a holistic project which will improve not only the production and marketing of the craft, but also the condition of the craft producers. In this context the help of modern management science deserve special mention.

(v) The empowerment of the artisans for cultivating their self-artistic skills and marketing of the products is also very necessary.

(vi) The marketing of *jari* products should be strengthened by creating a brand. At present there is no such "brand" in the market.

(vii) For entry into the market introduction of better designs in *jari* work is necessary as there is not much qualitative difference in designs of work supplied by various ustagars.

(C) Plan for Improvement of Quality of Life of the Artisans :

(i) The problems of *jari* embroidery and its embroiders have to be solved holistically. It requires strong organization among the artisans of all categories. Therefore, the artisans should be organized at first.

(ii) The ill effects of *jari* work among the child and young artisans are to be avoided by undertaking effective development programmes and their proper implementations.

(iii) Attempts have to be made to provide education to the child and adult artisans so that a better generation of artisans can be expected in future.

Appendices

ICSSR Research Project

The Embroidery (Jari) Works and the Embroiders of Bengal

Project Director : Prof. S. RAHIM MONDAL

UNIVERSITY OF NORTH BENGAL. DT. DARJEELING-734013

SCHEDULE-A

SCHEDULE FOR STUDY OF EMBROIDERS

1. Name : 2. Age : . 3. Sex
4. Duration of study in the village :
5. Nature of work :
6. Technical category :
7. *Age at jari* work :
8. Personal work history :
9. Period of training/apprenticeship :
10. Persons help to accept *jari* work :
11. Other economic activities :
12. Total weekly/monthly/income :
13. Economic position in the family :
14. Loan if any :
15. Education (details) :
16. Marital status :

17. If married : (a) Age : (b) Types : (c) Forms : (d) Payment : (e) Distance :
18. Caste/Ethnic/class background :
19. Religion :
20. Family background (details):
21. Interpersonal relations in the family :
22. Parent's occupation :
23. Membership in voluntary bodies :
24. Political participation (if any) :
25. Social relationships :
26. Religious practices and cultural habits :
27. Health care systems :
28. Time of leisure :
29. Forms of recreation :
30. House type :
31. Land owned :
32. Times of food and items of food :
33. Dress :
34. Future plans and aspirations :
35. The problems facing :
36. Suggestions prescribed :
37. Expectations :

Schedule-B

Schedule for *Jari* Workship and Household Production

1. What is the nature and type of *jari* work done ?
2. How many *jari* frames are in operation ?
3. What are the number of embroiders employed ?
4. What is the wage rate given to the workers ?
5. What about the nature of household productions ?
6. Who are the persons involved in household productions ?
7. What is the turnover per week/month ?
8. What is the range of cost of dress items embroidered ?
9. What is the cost of labour and raw material ?
10. What about the earning and profit per week/ month ?

Schedule-C
Schedule for Market Study
(Sellers and Suppliers)

1. What are the dress items with *jari* work usually do you sell ?
2. What are the price range of *jari* work items ?
3. On what occasions these dress materials do you sell ?
4. What are the peak and lean seasons ?
5. Where is the *jari* work done ?
6. How do you order and collect your requirements from the suppliers ?
7. What about the mode of payments to suppliers ?
8. What about the business terms between suppliers and workers ?
9. What is the profit margin of the suppliers ?
10. What is the profit margin of the sellers ?

Executive Summary, Findings and Policy Implications

1. **Title of the Research Project :** "The Embroidery (*jari*) works and the Embroiders of Bengal : An Anthropological Study of a Traditional Craft and an Occupational Group, with Special Reference to its Child Labour".

2. **Name and address of the Project Director :**

Dr. Sekh Rahim Mondal, Professor of Anthropology and Sociology Centre for Himalayan Studies, and also Professor in the Department of Anthropology University of North Bengal, Dist. Darjeeling, West Bengal, PIN - 734013.

INDIA

E.Mail : *rahimanthnbu@yahoo.co.in*

3. **Residence :**

Flat No. W281, North Bengal University Campus, P.O. North Bengal University, Dist. Darjeeling,

PIN - 734 430
Telephone :
(Res.) 0353-2581-123.
Mobile : 09434885831

About the Research Project

In order to retain the relevance in the first changing world, the social scientists have started to play a new role in the protection and conservation of cultural diversity and documentation of indigenous knowledge system. The traditional knowledge bases of the communities, specially the skills of indigenous arts and crafts of the world over are now being threatened and eroded by growing tide of modern mechanized technification and cultural homogenization of the planet. Under such a situation protection of cultural diversity as well as artistic heritage of folk and rural communities is very much necessary both for economic as well as for socio-cultural importance.

Traditional arts and crafts have been the very core of Indian civilization since time immemorial. The continuation of these traditional and indigenous skills are not only the nation's pride but have significant contributions in economic well being of the people as well as culture and civilization of the country. Since agriculture and large scale mechanized industries failed to provide full employment in India, so a section of less privileged people in rural and urban areas have to resort to various kinds of self employment and entrepreneurial activities for their survival. These include their involvement in marginally lucrative cottage industries like hand embroidery of *jari* work and various other indigenous craft works. But unfortunately research studies on traditional arts and crafts and small-scale entrepreneurial activities in India are rather very scanty.

Jari work is an important unorganized sector of artistic craft production. It is one such home industry and small-scale entrepreneurship which has a long tradition in Indian economy and culture. *Jari* work is a kind of hand-embroidery using gold/silver coloured metalic thread and other designing materials for designing on various dress items like ghagra-chunni, churidar, sari, jacket, veil and other clothing's. The craft of *jari* embroidery is said to be originated in Iran, but later propagated and developed in India during the medieval epa. Earlier this artsitic craft was liked by the aristocrats, but today it is gaining much popularity among the common masses.

Considering the unemployment problem in India and socio-cultural significance of the craft, it is necessary to preserve and encourage the *jari* embroidery industry. The ill effects of craft production on the life of the craft makers needs to be removed. For which development of the production system of this craft and life of the craft makers are very essential. All these require a thorough knowledge about the craft and the craft makers. But due to lack of empirical data we do not have much knowledge about this artistic craft and the artisans. There seems to be a big research gap on this subject. All these enableme to take up the study of hand embroidery (*jari* work) as a traditional Indian craft and the embroiders (*jari* artisans) as an occupational group of this country.

3. Aims of the Study

The basic aims of this study is to examine the social framework of *jari* work for formulating strategies to develop this craft and also to improve the quality of life of the artisans. To fulfil the above aims the basic objectives of this research are noted below :

4. Objectives of the Study

The specific objectives of this study are as follows :

1. To find out the manufacturing process i.e. the tools and technology as well as the division of labour involved in this artistic craft of hand embroidery (*jari* work).
2. To examine the structure and organizational aspects of the craft production.
3. To analyze the entrepreneurial activities and employer-employee relations around production system and marketing of *jari* craft.
4. To highlight the economic, social and cultural importance of *jari* embroidery.
5. To enquire the social background of entrepreneurs of *jari* embroidery industry.
6. To examine the economic, social and cultural life of the *jari* artisans.
7. To highlight the impact of *jari* work in village society.
8. To explore the nature, extent and problems of child labour involved in *jari* embroidery work

9. To assess the problems and to identify the bottlenecks in development of the *jari* embroidery industry.
10. To formulate strategies towards improvement of the *jari* craft and the life of the craft makers.

6. Significance of the Study :

The main purpose of this study are :

1. The study shall help in documentation of technology and indigenous knowledge system of the traditional artistic craft of hand (*jari*) embroidery.
2. The study shall help to delineate the problems and prospects of this Craft and the craft producers.
3. The result of the study shall help to evolve some strategies for growth of this craft and development of craft makers.

7. Methodology

Since this research project involved an in-depth study of hand embroidery (*jari*) work and socio-economic life of the workers, the study has been carried out in a holistic manner on the basis of structural-functional approach. It is purely an exploratory study with diagnostic outlook in some cases. The comparative method both synchronic and diachronic over space (place) and time (generation) have been adopted for understanding the present situation of this craft and craft-makers and the changes those have taken place among them from past to present context. For this research both qualitative and quantitative facts have been used. The facts are presented through descriptive and analytical manners.

This is an empirical study. Both secondary and primary data were collected by reviewing the published/unpublished materials and through field study. The field techniques used for data collection were interview, key informant's interview, focused group interview, case studies and observation. To obtain comprehensive data standard interview schedules were also used. The fieldwork was conducted between June, 1998 to December, 1999.

In this study 1 have tried to present a profile of *jari* embroidery as an artistic craft and the embroiders as an artisan group. As a part of these endeavour, I have dealt on the various facts of technology and economics of the craft and socio-economic life of the craft producers. For several months I have studied the embroiders at work, mixed with them, ascertained their attitudes to different social and cultural matters. As it is a detailed enquiry on a traditional Indian craft and the craft-makers, so research was conducted in places where the artistic skill of *jari* embroidery is highly prevalent among a group of people since very past. Thus four *jari* artisan villages of the district of Howrah in West Bengal were selected for the field study. The name of the villages are Dakshin Korola, Uttar Dhulagori, Sahapur and Paschim-Bauria located in the police stations of Damjur, Sankrail, Panchla and Bauria respectively. These localities are very famous for *jari* embroidery not only in Bengal, but also in the country as well.

Both extensive as well as intensive field works were conducted in those selected villages for data collection. Conventional anthropological tools and techniques were used for data collection. Collected data were processed after necessary checking and editing. Tabulation was done manually.

The quantitative data were analyzed by adopting simple statistical methods consisting calculation of percentage and average. While the qualitative facts were explained systematically and analytically.

SUMMARY OF THE FINDINGS

1. *Jari* work is a kind of hand embroidery using gold or silver coloured threads and some other glossy materials for designing on various dresses and other cloth items.
2. In India *jari* embroidery is highly prevalent in Rajasthan, Delhi, Mumbai, Kolkata and their hinterlands.
3. The district of Howrah in West Bengal is considered to be the largest center of best *jari* designers in the country.
4. *Jari* work (embroidery) are of various types like *arirkaj, jarirkaj, badgerkaj* and *rakhirkaj* etc.
5. The most important materials used in *jari* work are *kasap, tiki, resamdouri, sifandouri, builen, dobka, chir, moti, pipe, kutri, makmal, gulli* and other glossy things.
6. The most common tools require for *jari* work are a rectangular wooden frame (*dhadda*), niddle, scissors and file.

7. The most important dress items on which the artisans doing embroidery designing are *sari, ghagra-chunni, churidar*, jacket, *kurta, dopatta*, etc.
8. The manufacturing of *jari* embroidery is done both in workshops and in individual artisan households.
9. The traders or *mahajans* of the city exclusively controls the business of *jari* embroidery products. Below the *mahajans*, there are also middlemen called *ustagers*. Under the *ustagers* there are several *jari* artisans.
10. *Jari* artisans are of three categories viz., master artisan (*darji*), skilled artisan (*karigar*) and apprentices (*majurs*).
11. The artisans are both men and women as well as boys and girls.
12. The ustagars are considered to be the entrepreneurs of *jari* embroidery industry. They collect orders from the *mahajans*, prepare the designs, provide embroidery materials, engage the artisans to produce the craft and finally supply the products to the traders.
13. The *jari* artisans (embroiders) constitute an occupational group. Among the embroiders there are aged, youth, maiden and child artisans.
14. The majority of *jari* artisans are Muslims; however, there are some non-Muslima artisans too.

15. The overwhelming majority of *jari* artisans are between the age-group of 16-40 years. Among them there are more males and few females.
16. The craft of *jari* embroidery provide employment to many people.
17. The *jari* artisans do not constitute a homogeneous economic group. There is wide disparity in incomes among different categories of persons involved with this craft production.
18. *The jari* embroidery is an enterprise to many artisan families.
19. The average family size of *jari* artisans constituting of 7 persons. Both joint and nuclear families are noted among them.
20. The mean age at marriage of the male and female *jari* artisans is 23 years and 17 years respectively.
21. The educational level of *jari* artisans are significantly very low. Among them 36.06% having primary, 27.89% secondary, 7.48% higher secondary and only 2.04% graduate levels of education.
22. The young *jari* artisans are mostly the school dropouts.
23. Among child *jari* artisans only 31.82% are still attending school, but their attendance is of irregular nature.
24. Among *jari* artisans there are some girls and women (16.54%).

25. The women *jari* artisans are usually the widows or separated or divorced ladies.
26. The girls and women artisans are mostly working in their respective households. They, exclusively depend on male members of their family for receiving orders from the *ustagars*.
27. Owing to isolation and seclusion, the women *jari* artisans are deprived in many ways.
28. Recently an attempt has been made by a voluntary body (NGO) for economic empowerment of women through *jari* work. Some woman artisans of Sahapur village are benefited out of this novel attempt.
29. *Jari* work is a labour intensive, small and home industry to which participation of child labour is very conspicuous.
30. In field situation, among the *jari* workers 14.97% was child labourers.
31. The chil *jari* labourers were either engaged in workshops or household production.
32. The *ustagars* (entrepreneurs) those who engaged child labours in their workshops do not considered it as exploitation but regarded as a protection.
33. The parents have the feeling that it is quite normal for a poor family to utilize the child labour for earning to support their meagre income.
34. The parents opine that considering the problem of future unemployment it is their

social responsibility to engage children in *jari* work at an early age.

35. The child labourers of *jari* work have an educational background of primary and secondary levels.
36. Among child *jari* labourers 68.18% are school dropouts and remaining 31.82 percent irregularly attending school.
37. The work schedule of *jari* embroiders working in workshops is about 10 hours in a day.
38. Although the *jari* embroiders in general have low educational status, yet they acquired the artistic skill of *jari* embroidery very minutely from their kin's and friends.
39. The family environment played a major role in developing a congenial atmosphere for the growth of *jari* work as an occupation as well as an artistic craft production.
40. Inter-village differences in *jari* work are noted. In Dakshin Korola and Uttar Dhulagori *ari* work is prevalent. While in Paschim Bauria and Sahapur *jari* work is practiced. The embroiders of former two villages are aged and youths, while, in latter two villages the embroiders are youths and child.
41. The social position of *ari* and *jari* embroiders is somewhat low in all the four villages under study.
42. Due to socio-economic backwardness the *jari* artisans have failed to develop their craft

producing activities and facing problems to improve their social position.

43. The low level of education and lack of contact of the *jari* artisans lead them to live in isolation. These generated a conservative and undemonstrative attitude among them towards life and work lacking enthusiasm and quest of nobility.

44. The monotonous nature of work, low levels of living and popular nature of recreation affects the psychology, personality and quality of life of the artisans.

45. The *jari* embroidery work has an adverse effect on health of the artisans.

46. Most of the *jari* artisans are suffering from Rheumatism, loss of eyesight and indigestion.

47. *Jari* embroidery is a labour intensive industry and unorganized sector of production. The work is highly seasonal. It is usually difficult for an experienced artisan to perform his artistic work freely above the age of 40 years involvement of child labour is also conspicuous in this work. All these creating problems to sustain the life of the artisans.

48. The traditional craft of *jari* work has economic, social and cultural relevance. It stands for the continuity of an old craft and artistic heritage of India. The artisans of *jari* work and their entire production system is guided essentially by verbal testimonies. This artistic performance has been continuing as a oral tradition of india.

Recommendations :

1. Considering the economic and socio-cultural importance it is necessary to preserve and encourage this small-scale entrepreneurship of *jari* work.
2. Proper documentation of the system of this artistic craft production is an urgent need.
3. The problems of the *jari* craft and the craft makers have to be solved through proper planning and management.
4. Formation of some kind of co-operative is essential for long term feasibility of this craft production.
5. To form a co-operative it is necessary to organize the artisans (*karigars*) as well as the entrepreneurs (*ustagars*) of a particular locality.
6. The networking system between artisans (*karigars*), entrepreneurs (*ustagars*) and traders (*Mahajans*) should be developed and strengthened.
7. An arrangement should be made to provide bank loans to the needy entrepreneurs and artisans of this craft production.
8. For the future of *jari* embroidery industry, the most important thing which should be considered is the development of quality of the craft. It is necessary to invent the new designs of embroidery work for the sake of wider and global market.

9. The problem of seasonality in *jari* work have to be tackled through diversification of *jari* designs not only on male and female garments but also on other cloth items.
10. On the part of the artisans it is necessary to constitute a dealer network at the village level to get an entry into the market.
11. The income level of the artisans can be improved if number of stages involved in distribution network of production system is reduced.
12. Since manufacturing of *jari* crafts done both in the workshop and also in the individual artisan households, so these two sectors should be integrated.
13. In case of household production, work is done mainly by the female artisans, who are also required to do various other domestic works. Thus, this sector needs to be organized properly.
14. Training programme for male and female artisans are very necessary for improving their skills of production.
15. For greater prospect of *jari* craft more domestic and export markets should be explored and for which diversification of *jari* designing on various dress and other items is very essential.
16. The marketing of the products shall be benefited much if the entrepreneurs (*ustagars*) establish their contacts directly with the retailers and whole sellers.

17. The marketing of *jari* designed products should be strengthened through creating a “brand”.
18. Empowerment of artisans for cultivating their self-artistic motives of production and marketing of products are very much desirable.
19. For improving income, working condition, and levels of living of the artisans it is necessary to organize them in a planned manner.
20. Exploitation of the artisans as well as the entrepreneurs by various middlemen in different stages of production and marketing of products should be eliminated
21. The ill effects of *jari* work among the artisans, specially among the children and the youths should be avoided by undertaking effective development programes and their implementations by the government and the voluntary bodies (NGO).
22. Attempts should be made to provide education among the child and adult *jari* artisans, so that a better generation of artisans may be expected in future.

References

Ahuja, Ram, 1997 — *Social Problems in India*, Jaipur : Rawat Publications.

Approach Paper to Nineth Five Year Plan — (1997-2002), Government of India.

Begum Rokaiya, 1995: — "Cottage Industry and the Rural Women. The Case of Coir and *Jari* Work in West Bengal, India" in A.U., Khan and M.A., Baqee (eds.) *Commercial Activity, Women and Ecology,* Dhaka : Bangladesh Geographical Society.

Dobb, Maurice, 1976 — *Studies in the Development of Capitalism,* New York : International Publishers, (First edition 1947).

Fyfe Al.ec, 1993 — *Child Labour A Guide to Project Design :* Geneva : International Labour Office.

Goody, Jack, 1996 — *The East in the West*, Cambridge: Cambridge University Press.

Heberer, Thomas, 1998 — "Entrepreneurs in China and Vietnam and their Impact on Social and Political Change", Paper presented to the Second Workshop on Small and Medium-Scale Entrepreneurship in Asia and Europe Compared: Organizations, Business Behaviour and the State, 10-12 December, 1998, Kuala-Lampur, Malaysia.

Kumar, Vinod, 1996 "Entrepreneur Development in Traditional Food Products" in *Laghu Udyog Samachar,* November, 1996.

Kumar, S.A. 1988 *Zari Workers.in. West Bengal,* Calcutta : Action Aid.

Manna, Ashok, 1994 *"Jarigram" Sananda,* October, 1994, pp. 55-60.

Mittal, Mukta, 1992 *Child Labour in Unorganized Sector,* New Delhi: Sterling Publishers.

Mondal, Sekh Rahim, 1979 "*Jari* Work in a Muslim Village" in *Khadi Gramodyog,* Vol. 25, No. 8, May 1979.

Mondal, Sekh Rahim, 2006a, "*Muslim Jari*" embroiders or West Bengal: Some observations on their economy, identity and Entrepreneurial Behvaviour", in A. Waheed (Ed.) *Muslim Artisan, Craftsmen and Traders,* New Delhi : Icon Publications Pvt. Ltd.

Mondal Sekh Rahim, 2006b "Muslim Women *Jari* Embroiders of West Bengal-Their Role, Status and Empowerment issues", in *Islam and Muslim Societies,* Vol. 2, No. 2, 2006, pp. 377-389.

Mukhopadhayay, K.K., 1995 "Girl Prostitution in India", in *Social Change* Vol. 25, Nos. 2 & 3, 199.

Nazmul Karim, A.K. 198 *The Dynamics of Bangladesh Society,* New Delhi : Vikas Publishing House Pvt. Ltd.

Rullen, Mario, 1995 *Farms and Factories : Social Profile of Large Farmers and Rural Industrialists in West India,* Delhi: Oxford University Press.

Schumpeter, Joseph, A. 1936 *The Theory of Economic Development,* Cambridge.

Simmel, Georg, 1994 *Philosophie des Geldes,* Frankfurt.

Singh Surednra and K. Taori (eds.), 1993 Rural Industrialization - A Plan for the Seventh Five Years Plan (1985-90) Vol. 2 New Delhi : Vikas Publishing House Pvt. Ltd.

Sinha, K. Krishna, 1990 "Rationale Behind Rural Industries", in *Kurukeshetra,* Vol. 30(7), pp. 49-52.

Singh, I.S. 1992 Child Labour, New Delhi : Oxford Publishing Company.

Solanki, S.S. 1993 "Modern Technology and the Indian Rural Artisans", in *Science, Technology and Development,* Vol. 2, No. 3. Frank Case, London.

Tripathy, S.N. 1997 *Migrant Child Labour in India,* New Delhi : Mohit Publications.

Index

N